Rhyme Time BLOCKS

Rita Denenberg

Located in Paducah, Kentucky, the American Quilter's Society (AQS) is dedicated to promoting the accomplishments of today's quilters. Through its publications and events, AQS strives to honor today's quiltmakers and their work and to inspire future creativity and innovation in quiltmaking.

EDITOR: BARBARA SMITH
BOOK DESIGN/ILLUSTRATIONS: LISA M. CLARK
COVER DESIGN: MICHAEL BUCKINGHAM
PHOTOGRAPHY: CHARLES R. LYNCH

Library of Congress Cataloging-in-Publication Data

Denenberg, Rita

    Rhyme time blocks / Rita Denenberg

    p. cm.

    ISBN 1-57432-752-6

1. Appliqué–Patterns. 2. Machine appliqué–Patterns.   3. Nursery rhymes in art.
4. Children's quilts. I. Title.

    TT779.D45   2000

746.46'041–dc21   00-009344

                                              CIP

Contents

Acknowledgments

Thank you to my dearest husband, Martin, who
supported and encouraged me in this endeavor and
who has always stood by me during my quilting career.
His patience and love have helped
all my dreams come true.

I want to thank Penny McMorris and Dean Neumann,
who gave me the opportunity to work with them
as part of their computer program in which many
of these blocks were designed.

I also want to thank Mickie Swall of the RCTQ network
group on the Internet. It was Mickie who first gave
me the idea to write a book, promising
to purchase the first copy.

Introduction

Many of us have delighted our children with charming nursery rhymes. For those who want to delight them even more, here are some block patterns you can make to give a child a quilt of happy memories. Imagine your child snuggling into this gift of love as you read these delightful little rhymes.

This book is designed for quilters of all skill levels. It starts with fairly simple blocks and progresses to those with more detail. By the time you reach Lesson 9, you will have learned a lot about appliquéing, and you will see how patterns can be made with a minimum of tracing and marking.

Lesson 10 shows you how to trim the blocks and gives you some ideas for setting the blocks into quilts of various sizes. You may want to make only one large block to use as a wallhanging, or perhaps you will want to include all the blocks in one quilt. Hopefully, you will use all the lessons, so that, by the time you have completed them, you will have the techniques to make the bonus blocks at the back of the book.

If you are an expectant mother, this book will have you making quilts for your precious baby while you anticipate his or her arrival. If you are a mother of young children, these patterns will give you the opportunity to share your quilting ability with your children. Show them the patterns and read them the rhymes. After making a block, you can give your child the pattern to color or copy the coloring pages at the back of the book. If you're a grandmother, you can make a special quilt for your grandchildren. They will always remember "Granny made this special for me."

Today, many of the rhymes may be deemed politically incorrect, but they are as traditional as our cherished quilts. The ones presented here are as I remember them from my childhood. I hope you enjoy them and enjoy making these blocks.

Part 1 — General Instructions

SUPPLIES

Before you begin, you will need the following supplies:

BACKGROUND FABRIC:
Prewashed and heavily starched 100% cotton fabric. Cotton is preferred because it is more manageable for appliqué where you will be turning a lot of curves. Polyesters and blends are less forgiving. A solid, pastel background is recommended.

APPLIQUÉ FABRIC:
Prewashed, starched, and pressed 100% cotton fabric. These can be solids or prints.

THREAD:
100% cotton thread matching the appliqué fabric. If you cannot get an exact match, choose a shade darker than the appliqué fabric.

NEEDLES:
Sharps #11, millinery, or beading needles are best.

FABRIC GLUE STICK:
Do not confuse it with a glue gun. It is glue in a tube, which can be purchased in any dry goods department store. The glue stick is used in lieu of pins. It is harmless to fabric and washes out.

EMBROIDERY FLOSS:
For fine details that are too small for appliqué.

FREEZER PAPER:
Freezer paper can be used for all the projects. It is easy to use for tracing because you can see a dark image beneath it. You will be making two freezer-paper patterns: a copy of the whole pattern as it appears in the book and a reverse copy to be cut apart and ironed on the wrong side of your fabric.

Freezer paper is inexpensive and can be purchased in any large food store. Look for the type that has a shiny waxed side. The waxed side will stick to fabric when the paper is ironed on.

LIGHT BOX:
If none is available to you, you could use a window or patio door, which, of course, will limit you to daylight hours. You can also improvise by using a glass-topped table with a lamp underneath.

STARCH:
Use bottled liquid starch rather than spray starch.

SMALL CUP:
Smaller amounts of starch are easier to use. Unused starch can be poured back into the bottle.

SHARP PENCIL OR MECHANICAL PENCIL:
For tracing and marking.

FUSIBLE WEB:
For adhering the appliqué pieces to the background fabric.

STABILIZER:
For machine embroidery and machine appliqué.

INVISIBLE THREAD:
For machine blind stitch appliqué.

MASKING TAPE:
To hold fabric and freezer paper while tracing. The tape can be used several times before discarding.

SMALL SHARP SCISSORS:
For trimming allowances and cutting thread.

MACHINE APPLIQUÉ FOOT:
An open-toed foot will enable you to see where you are stitching.

EMBROIDERY HOOP:
To hold blocks while adding details.

PREPARING FREEZER PAPER WHOLE PATTERN

All the full-sized appliqué patterns have been divided into two sections, as shown by dotted lines, and the center of each pattern has been marked with a cross in a circle.

The first step is to cut a 12" square of freezer paper for pattern transfer. This pattern will be referred to as the "whole pattern." Fold the paper in half, shiny side in. Open the paper and fold it in half in the other direction (Figure 1). Making each fold separately prevents the paper from becoming distorted. To make the folds easier to see for later steps, mark them as shown in Figure 2.

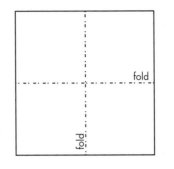
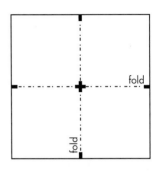

Fig. 1. Fold the paper in half. Open the paper and fold it again in the other direction.

Fig. 2. Mark the center of the pattern with a small cross and mark the folds at the edges.

Use the following method to transfer the appliqué pattern to the folded freezer paper: Lay the appropriate half of the freezer paper dull side up on the pattern and align the *center* of the paper with the *center* of the pattern (the paper's fold lines will not always match those on the fabric). Trace that section. Move the paper as needed to trace the other section.

PREPARING BACKGROUND SQUARES

Because appliquéing can change a block's dimensions, start with a fabric piece larger than the desired finished size. Therefore, cut the background squares 14". The blocks will be trimmed to 12½", including seam allowances, after being appliquéd.

Fold the fabric background square in half, and in half again, as you did the freezer paper. Finger press the fold each time.

Place the whole pattern, drawn side up, on a light source and tape it down at the corners. Matching centers and folds, place the background square, right side up, over the pattern, and tape the corners. Because the fabric piece is larger than the paper pattern, you should have an even amount of overlap on all four sides (Figure 3). Trace the pattern lightly to indicate appliqué placement.

Fig. 3. Tape the whole pattern to the light source; position the fabric over the pattern, allowing equal overlap on all four sides.

PREPARING REVERSE PATTERN FOR APPLIQUÉS

After tracing the pattern on the background square, tape the whole pattern face down on the light source. Tape another 12" square of freezer paper over it, dull side up. Trace the pattern to produce the reverse of the design. This reverse tracing is your cutting pattern for making the appliqué pieces. Because the appliqués will be pressed to the wrong side of the fabric, if they are not reversed, they will turn out backward (Figure 4). Trace everything carefully because this step will affect the appearance of the finished appliqué.

Cut the reverse freezer paper pattern pieces apart as you use them. You will add turn-under allowances as you cut your fabric pieces.

Press the reverse pattern pieces shiny side down on the wrong side of the fabric. Cut the patches out with a scant ¼" turn-under allowance all the way around. No need to measure.

Freezer paper patterns can be used numerous times, so if you make an error in cutting the fabric, just move the pattern piece and press in place again.

STARCH AND TURN METHOD

If you are unfamiliar with freezer paper appliqué, you may want to use the following directions for practice:

Cut a shape out of freezer paper. Iron it shiny side down to the wrong side of a piece of fabric. The

appliqué shape will end up being reversed. Cut out the fabric piece with a scant ¼" turn-under allowance all the way around. There's no need to measure. With the paper side face up, put a small amount of liquid starch in a small bowl. With your finger, dab a bit of the starch onto the allowance. Using the tip of an iron and the edge of the sole plate near the tip, turn the allowances toward the paper. The edge of the freezer paper will be your guide for turning the allowance.

Incorrect

Correct

Fig. 4. If the pattern is not reversed, the letter will be backward.

Continue turning the allowance in increments all the way around the piece, clipping the allowances where necessary, so the fabric lies flat. After all the edges have been pressed and they have dried, remove the paper. Use a glue stick and dab around the edge of the piece and set it in place on the background square. The glue will hold the piece in place rather than having to use pins.

LABELING YOUR QUILT

Photocopy one of the nursery rhyme scrolls (reduce if necessary) to use as your quilt label. Include your name, date completed, and the name of the new quilt owner. Embroider or use fabric marking pens and appliqué the label to the quilt back after quilting and binding.

Part 2

Nursery
Rhyme
Blocks

Twinkle Twinkle, Little Star

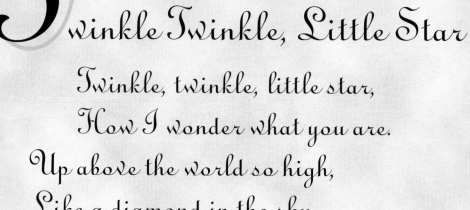

Twinkle, twinkle, little star,
How I wonder what you are.
Up above the world so high,
Like a diamond in the sky.
Twinkle, twinkle, little star,
How I wonder what you are.

Lesson 1
TURNING ALLOWANCES
BLIND STITCH BY HAND

Techniques to Use
General Instructions (pages 7–8)
Preparing freezer paper whole pattern
Preparing background square
Preparing reverse pattern for appliqués
Starch and turn method

Make a whole and a reverse pattern on 12" squares of freezer paper. Make a separate reverse pattern of the hat and brim.

Cut a 14" fabric square for the background. Press the reverse pattern, shiny side down, on the back of the square. Lightly trace the star outline on the right side of the square.

Cut out the reverse freezer paper star by cutting through the brim and hat since you have a duplicate of these. Press the shiny side of the paper to the wrong side of the star fabric.

Cut out the fabric star, leaving approximately a ¼" turn-under allowance. There is no need to measure. Clip into the inside angles of the star as shown in Figure 1.

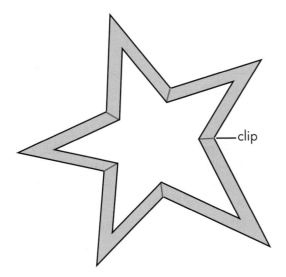

Fig. 1. Clip angles to within a thread or two of the fold line.

TURNING ALLOWANCES:

Leave the paper pattern in place. With your finger, dab the allowance at each star point with starch. Turn the allowances against the paper and press with the tip and edge of the iron's sole plate (Figure 2). Trim off point after it has been turned.

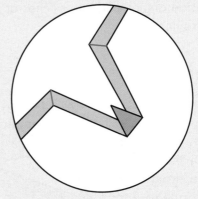

Fig. 2. Turn the allowance at each star tip.

Similarly, turn the allowances along the sides of the star points. Trim protrusions, if necessary, to keep them from interfering with the next fold (Figure 3) or from showing beyond the edge of the star (Figure 4).

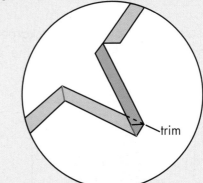

Fig. 3. Turn and press one side of the point. Trim as necessary.

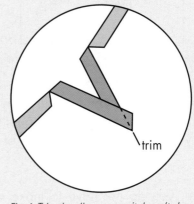

Fig. 4. Trim the allowance so it doesn't show.

Using a glue stick, dab, not drag, the stick on the allowances of the star. If you drag the glue stick, it will distort the fabric. Glue the star in place on the background square; let the glue dry completely.

Using a thread that matches the star, appliqué it to the block with a blind stitch. Take two to three stitches in the inside angles and two stitches at the points to prevent fraying.

BLIND STITCH BY HAND:

The blind stitch is achieved by bringing the needle up through the edge of the appliqué and catching only one or two threads in the fold. Direct the needle straight down into the background. Return the needle about 1/16"–1/8" away from the previous stitch so the stitches are as tiny as possible (Figure 5).

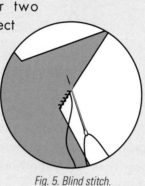

Fig. 5. Blind stitch.

With small scissors, cut away the background from beneath the star, 1/8"–1/4" away from the stitching (Figure 6).

Fig. 6. On the back of the block, cut away the background underneath the star.

Carefully cut out both eyes (whole) from the used star pattern. Do not cut the irises and pupils yet. Iron the paper eye pieces to the wrong side of the white fabric.

If you notice, you do not have to make additional patterns for the eyes because the freezer paper patterns can be used several times.

As you did with the star, cut around the patterns with a 1/4" turn-under allowance. Clip the allowance at intervals and turn it under with the starch and glue method. Remove the paper pattern and re-press. Glue the all-white eyes in place and blind stitch (Figure 7).

Fig. 7. Stitch white circles in place.

Cut the iris patterns from the whole-eye patterns just used. Do not cut the pupils yet. Press the patterns to the wrong side of the iris fabric and cut out the appliqué pieces with turn-under allowances.

Turn the allowances as before. Remove the patterns and press. Glue and stitch the irises in place on the white eyes (Figure 8).

Cut the pupils from the just-used patterns and repeat the steps for appliquéing them in place (Figure 9).

Fig. 8. Stitch irises in place.   Fig. 9. Add pupils.

Cut the mouth pattern from the star pattern. Press the pattern to the wrong side of the red fabric. Trace the inside of the mouth on the right side of the fabric. Cut around the outside of the mouth, making sure to include the turn-under allowance. Turn the allowance on the outside of the mouth.

Dab the glue stick on the turned allowance and glue the mouth to a small piece of white fabric the size of the lips. Let the piece dry but don't appliqué it yet.

Twinkle Twinkle, Little Star

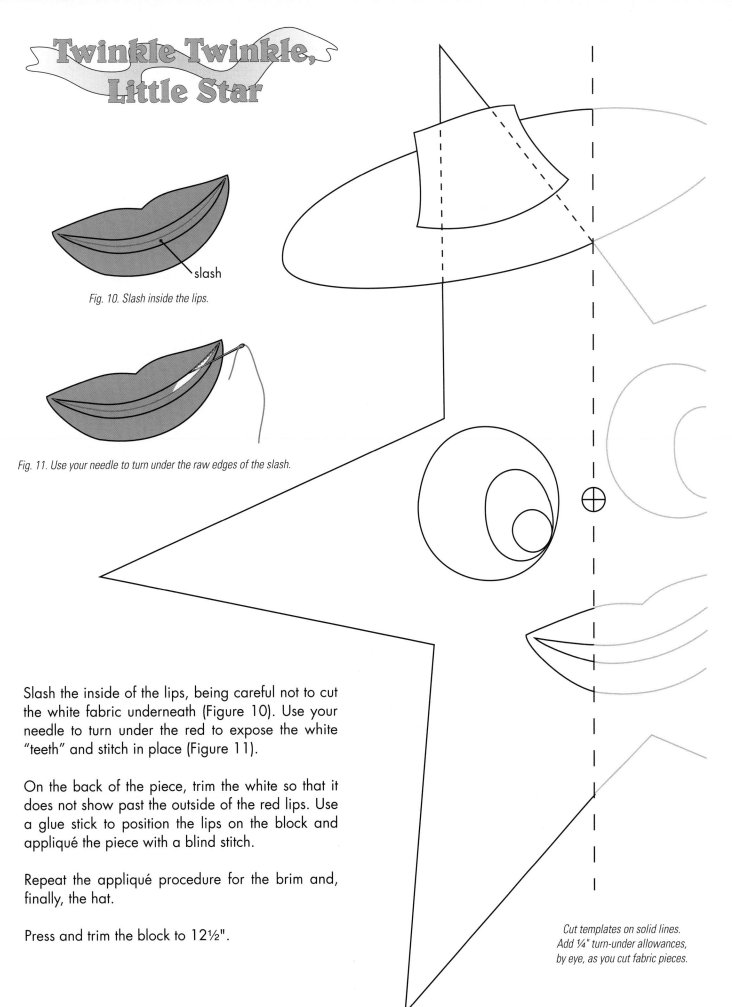

slash

Fig. 10. Slash inside the lips.

Fig. 11. Use your needle to turn under the raw edges of the slash.

Slash the inside of the lips, being careful not to cut the white fabric underneath (Figure 10). Use your needle to turn under the red to expose the white "teeth" and stitch in place (Figure 11).

On the back of the piece, trim the white so that it does not show past the outside of the red lips. Use a glue stick to position the lips on the block and appliqué the piece with a blind stitch.

Repeat the appliqué procedure for the brim and, finally, the hat.

Press and trim the block to 12½".

Cut templates on solid lines.
Add ¼" turn-under allowances,
by eye, as you cut fabric pieces.

Twinkle Twinkle, Little Star

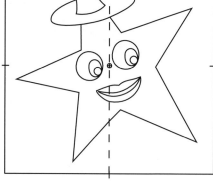

Cut templates on solid lines.
Add ¼" turn-under allowances,
by eye, as you cut fabric pieces.

Hey, Diddle Diddle

Hey, diddle diddle,

The cat and the fiddle,

The cow jumped over the moon.

The little dog laughed,

To see such sport,

And the dish ran away with the spoon.

Lesson 2
CUT AS YOU SEW
PERFECT CIRCLES

Techniques to Use
General Instructions (pages 7–8)
Preparing freezer paper whole pattern
Preparing background square
Preparing reverse patterns for appliqués
Starch and turn method

Lesson 1 (pages 11–13)
Turning allowances
Blind stitch by hand

Make a whole and a reverse pattern on 12" squares of freezer paper. Make a separate reverse pattern for the spoon.

Cut a 14" fabric square for the background. Press the reverse pattern, shiny side down, on the back of the square. Lightly trace the dish outline on the right side of the square to help position the appliqué piece.

Cut out the full circle reverse freezer paper pattern of the dish, cutting through the spoon; you already have a separate pattern for the spoon. Iron the dish pattern to the wrong side of the appliqué fabric.

Trace the eyes, nose, and mouth on the right side of the fabric. The dotted line in the middle of the mouth is a quilting line.

Cut out the dish, leaving a ¼" turn-under allowance by eye. Remove the template and position the dish on the background square. Pin or hand baste inside the traced line, not in the allowance.

CUT AS YOU SEW:
For the distance of about one inch, trim the allowance to ³⁄₁₆" (Figure 1). Needle-turn the allowance and blind stitch the section. Trim another inch of the allowance, turn and blind stitch again.

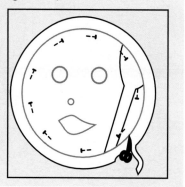

Fig. 1. Trim the allowance just before you needle-turn it.

PERFECT CIRCLES:
Cut a template for the whole eye. The ideal material for this template is a subscription card found in magazines.

Cut the fabric eye just a bit larger than the template, enough larger to sew a running stitch near the edge (Figure 2).

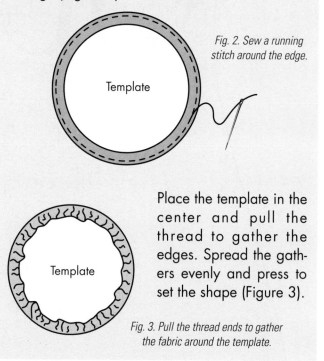

Fig. 2. Sew a running stitch around the edge.

Place the template in the center and pull the thread to gather the edges. Spread the gathers evenly and press to set the shape (Figure 3).

Fig. 3. Pull the thread ends to gather the fabric around the template.

Continue in this manner until the entire dish has been appliquéd to the background square. Cut away the background from under the appliquéd dish.

Remove the template and position the eye in place on the dish with a glue stick. Sew with a blind stitch (page 12). Use the same procedure for the pupils and the nose.

Cut the mouth pattern and iron it to the back of the fabric; starch, turn, and press.

Using a light source, trace the quilting line on the mouth, as designated by the dotted line on the pattern. Remove the pattern, dab the turned allowances with a glue stick, and glue the lips to the dish. Blind stitch the mouth in place.

Press the freezer paper pattern for the spoon to wrong side of the fabric and cut. Clip the inside curves; starch, turn, and press the edges.

Place the spoon over a light source and trace the eye and nose on the right side of the fabric. Appliqué the spoon with blind stitches. Use the instructions for perfect circles to make the eye and nose.

On the mouth, press the pattern on the wrong side of the fabric and cut. Position it in place and needle-turn, taking two extra stitches at the corners of the mouth.

Press and trim the block to 12½". Prepare the other three blocks of the rhyme using 14" background blocks and freezer paper and appliqué techniques.

Cut templates on solid lines.
Add ¼" turn-under allowances,
by eye, as you cut fabric pieces.

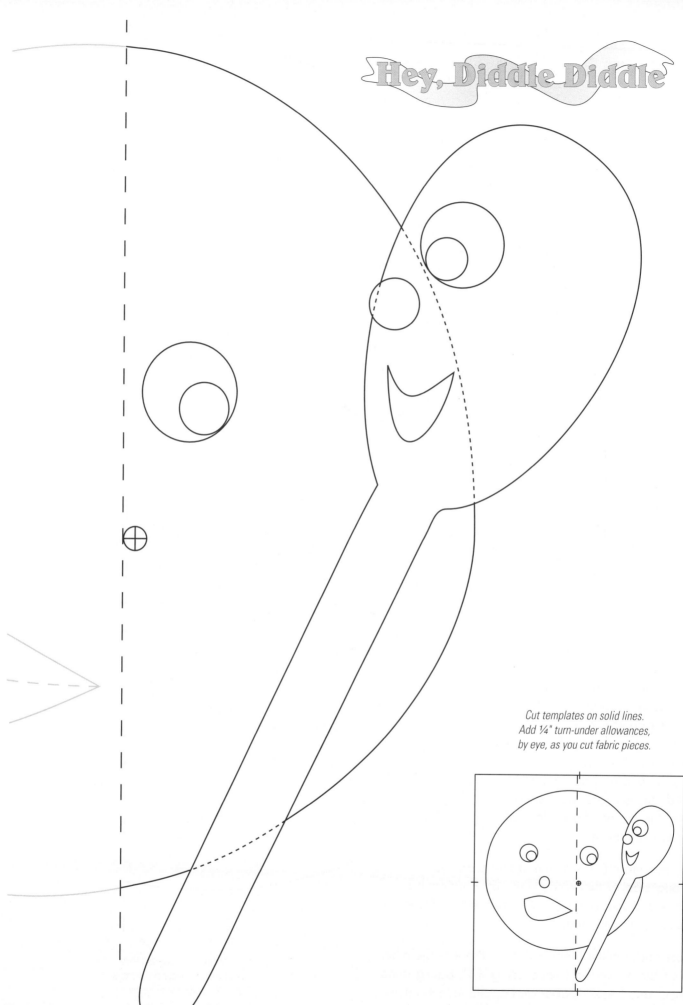

Hey, Diddle Diddle

Cut templates on solid lines.
Add ¼" turn-under allowances,
by eye, as you cut fabric pieces.

Rhyme Time Blocks ☙ Rita Denenberg

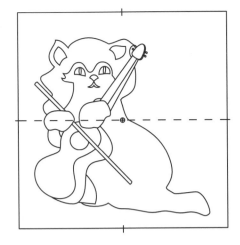

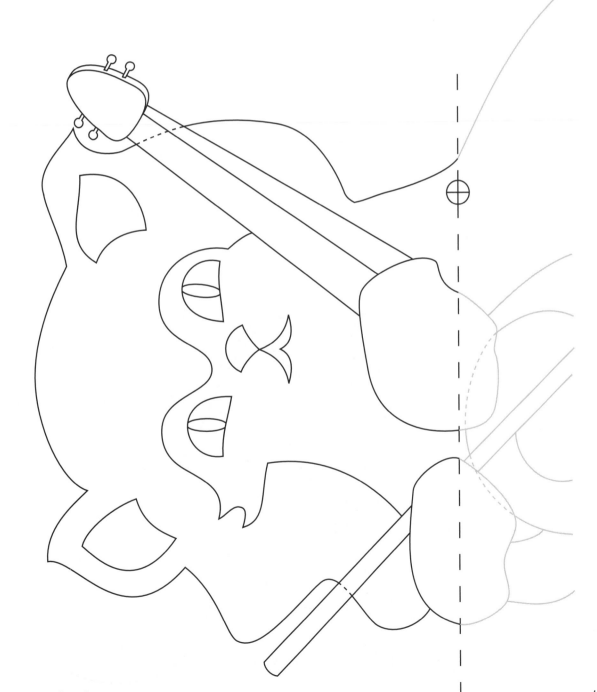

Hey, Diddle Diddle

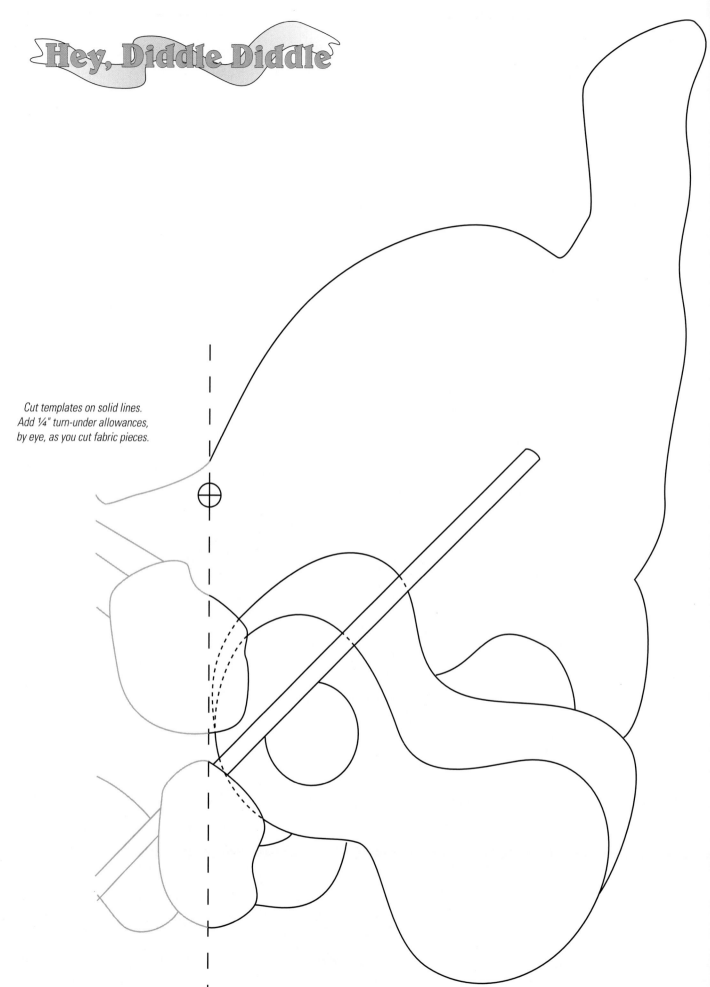

*Cut templates on solid lines.
Add ¼" turn-under allowances,
by eye, as you cut fabric pieces.*

Rhyme Time Blocks ❧ *Rita Denenberg*

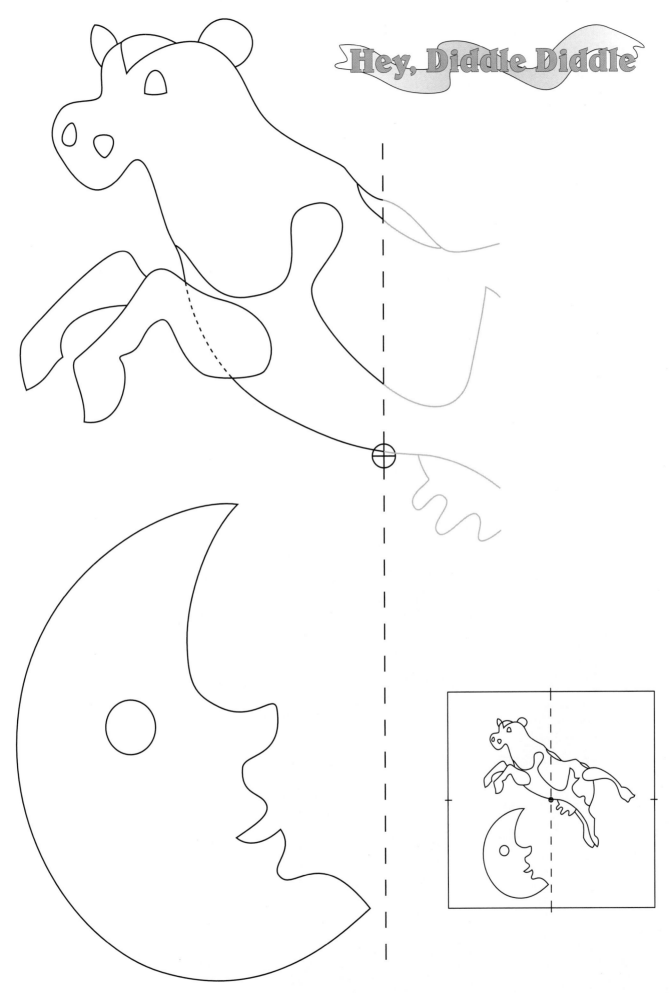

Cut templates on solid lines.
Add ¼" turn-under allowances,
by eye, as you cut fabric pieces.

Here is a sample of a wallhanging with 4 blocks. Add
your own twists such as quilting the rhyme, as shown
here in HEY DIDDLE DIDDLE by Rita Denenberg.

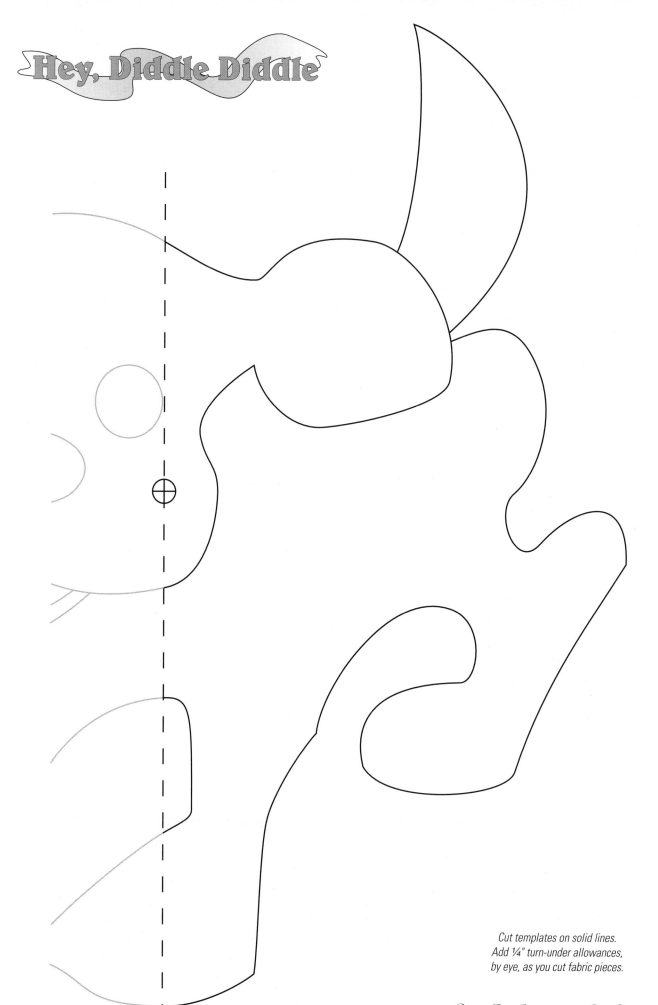

Hey, Diddle Diddle

*Cut templates on solid lines.
Add ¼" turn-under allowances,
by eye, as you cut fabric pieces.*

Rhyme Time Blocks � *Rita Denenberg*

Hickory Dickory Dock

Hickory dickory dock,
The mouse ran up the clock.
The clock struck one,
And down he run,
Hickory, dickory, dock.

Lesson 3

MACHINE APPLIQUÉ, SATIN STITCH
FUSED APPLIQUÉ
OVERLAPS

Techniques to Use
General Instructions (pages 7–8)
Preparing freezer paper whole pattern
Preparing background square
Preparing reverse pattern for appliqués
Starch and turn method

Lesson 1 (page 11)
Turning allowances

Make a whole and a reverse pattern on 12" squares of freezer paper. Make a separate reverse pattern of the mouse.

Cut a 14" fabric square for the background. Press the reverse pattern on the back of the square and trace the pattern lightly on the right side of the square. Trace the complete Roman numeral VI by extending the lines behind the mouse.

Remove the freezer paper pattern. Cut the frame from the pattern by cutting through the mouse. Press the frame pattern on the back of the frame fabric. Cut around the outside and inside of the frame, adding a ¼" allowance, by eye, as you cut. Turn the frame right side up and trace the seam lines on the fabric (Figure 1). Remove the pattern.

With both fabrics right side up, place the frame on the background square, using the tracing on the square as a guide. The frame's inside allowance will overlap the clock face. Use a glue stick to anchor the frame.

Cut out the reverse mouse pattern. Make separate reverse freezer paper patterns for the ears.

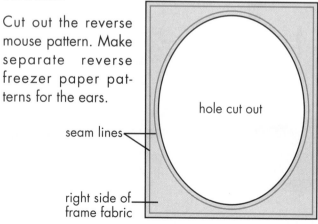

hole cut out

seam lines

right side of frame fabric

Fig. 1. Trace seam lines on front of fabric frame.

MACHINE APPLIQUÉ, SATIN STITCH:

Cut a piece of tear-away stabilizer a little larger than the frame. If a commercial stabilizer is not available, use typing paper. Place the stabilizer under the background square. With a sewing machine, run straight stitching on the seam lines along the inside and outside edges of the frame. Trim away the allowances close to the stitching lines (Figure 2).

Fig. 2. Stitch on the drawn seam lines. Trim allowances close to seam.

Use a narrow satin stitch to appliqué the inside and outside edges of the frame to the block. To begin the satin stitch, take a few stitches in place to lock the threads. Make sure your needle is in the down position before pivoting at the corners. Take a few stitches in place when ending. Cut the thread and remove the stabilizer. Trim away the background square from underneath the frame, leaving at least a ⅛" allowance.

FUSED APPLIQUÉ:

Trace all the Roman numerals on the dull side of a piece of fusible web. Keep the numerals fairly close together while tracing (Figure 3). Cut them apart after attaching the fusible web.

Fig. 3. Trace numerals close together on fusible web.

Following the manufacturer's directions, press the web piece to the appropriate fabric and cut out the numbers.

FUSED APPLIQUÉ cont.

Peel off the backing and press the appropriate numerals in position on the clock face. Use a narrow satin stitch to sew the numerals in place (Figure 4). Narrow the stitching as you approach the bottom of the Roman numeral V (Figure 5).

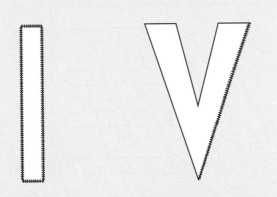

Fig. 4. Appliqué numerals with a narrow satin stitch.

Fig. 5. Use a narrower stitch width at the bottom of the V.

As an alternative, you may want to embroider the numerals instead of appliquéing them. Use two to three strands of embroidery floss, depending on how heavy you want the numerals to be.

For machine embroidery, it's a good idea to practice on a scrap first to make sure your choices for stitch width and length are correct. Place stabilizer in back of the area to be embroidered. Set the stitch width to match the width of the numerals.

Trace the reverse ears, including the pink inner portion of the front ear, on the matte side of a piece of fusible web. Do not cut the ears yet.

Press the fusible with the tracings onto the wrong side of the ear fabric.

Using an appliqué foot, with feed dogs engaged, you can satin stitch the outer edges with a narrow stitch width and a short stitch length. Sew around curves carefully. When the curve is too tight to continue sewing, put the needle down at the outer edge of the ear, release the presser foot, and turn the piece by hand.

Cut the inner ear from the reverse pattern and fuse it to the pink fabric, as described previously. Set aside.

OVERLAPS:

Cut out the ears, but leave a ¼" allowance on the bottom of the back ear. The head of the mouse will overlap this portion of the ear (Figure 6).

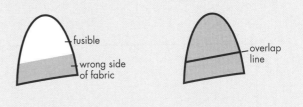

Fig. 6. Leave a ¼" allowance on the bottom of the back ear.

Fig. 7. Trace the overlap line.

Place the back ear right side up on a light source and trace the overlap line lightly with a pencil (Figure 7). Remove the backing and press in place on the background square.

Trace the reverse mouse body pattern on a piece of fusible web, and press the pattern to the wrong side of the appliqué fabric. Cut the mouse on the drawn lines.

Peel off the backing and fuse the mouse in place according to the directions for the fusible web.

Place stabilizer behind the work and machine appliqué with a narrow satin stitch, gradually narrowing the stitches as you reach the tail tip. Gradually widen the stitches as you sew toward the body making sure all the edges are enclosed. You may have to overlap the previous stitches for uniformity.

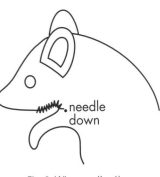

Fig. 8. When appliquéing or embroidering, keep needle down on inside edge before pivoting.

Trace the hands of the clock in one piece on the fusible and press on the wrong side of the fabric. Cut out the clock hands. Remove the backing and fuse in place with an iron. Stabilize and machine appliqué with satin stitching. Finish off with a hand satin-stitched eye for the mouse.

Press and trim the block to 12½".

Hickory Dickory Dock

Cut templates on solid lines.
Add ¼" turn-under allowances,
by eye, as you cut fabric pieces.

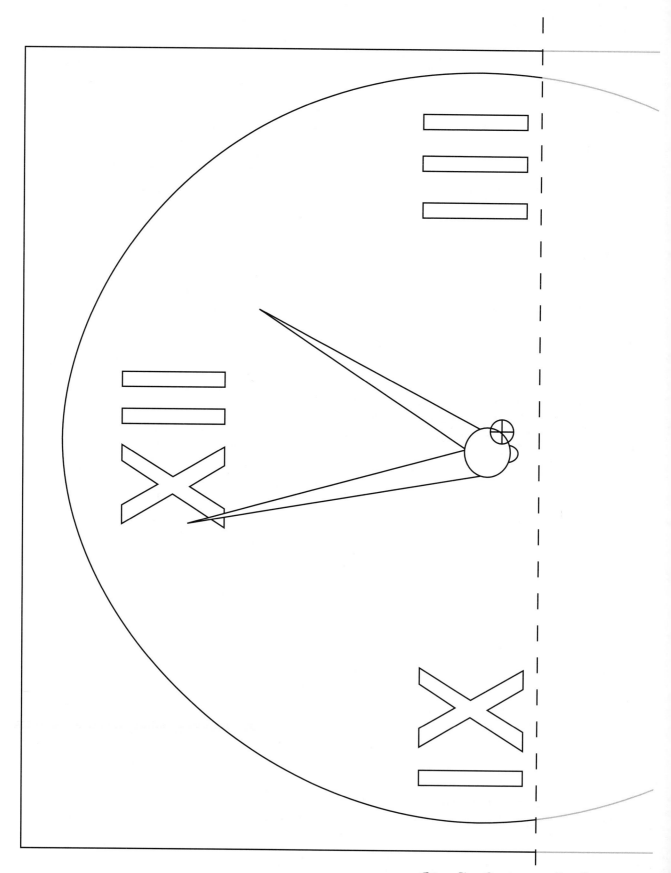

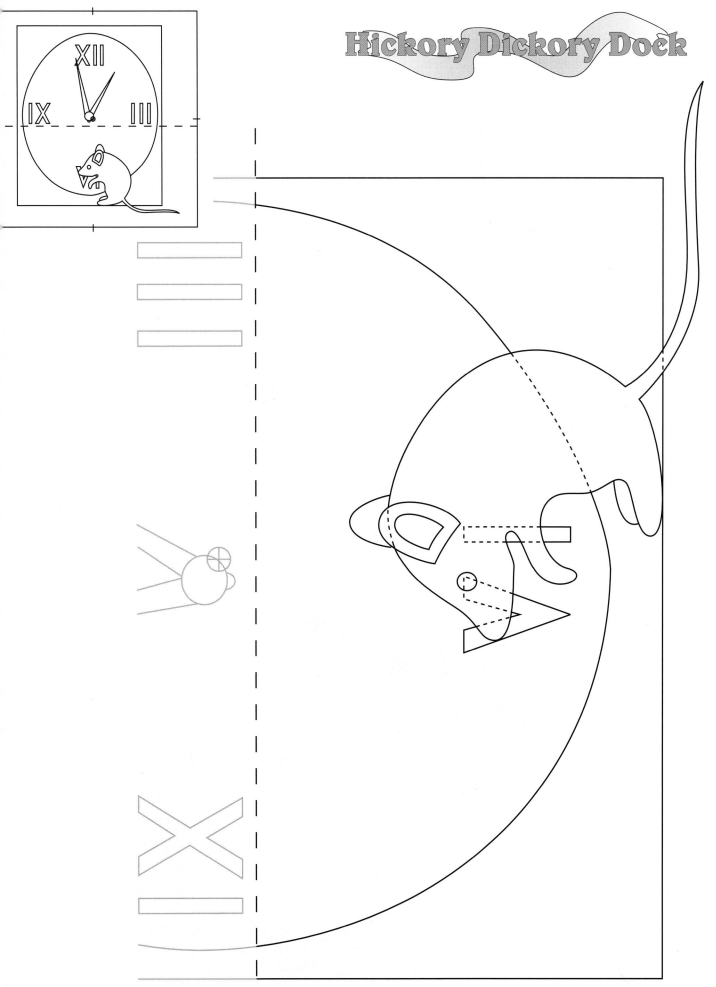

Hickory Dickory Dock

Rock-a-Bye, Baby

Rock-a-bye, baby,
In the tree top,
When the wind blows,
The cradle will rock.
When the bough breaks,
The cradle will fall.
Down will come baby,
Cradle and all.

Lesson 4
MACHINE APPLIQUÉ, BLIND STITCH
MORE OVERLAPS

Techniques to Use
General Instructions (pages 7–8)
Preparing freezer paper whole pattern
Preparing background square
Preparing reverse pattern for appliqués
Starch and turn method

Lesson 1 (page 11)
Turning allowances

Lesson 3 (pages 26–27)
Machine appliqué, satin stitch
Overlaps

Make a whole and a reverse pattern on 12" squares of freezer paper. Make another reverse tracing of the tree limb by drawing through the blanket and the leaf. Do the same with the head, hand, leg, and foot that are partially covered. Just make sure that the overlap will be covered by the other leg and foot as shown by the red in Figure 1.

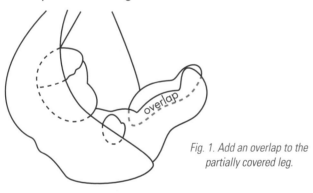

Fig. 1. Add an overlap to the partially covered leg.

Add overlaps to the back portion of the blanket, one where the blanket goes behind the tree branch, and another behind the baby.

Cut a 14" fabric square for the background. Press the reverse pattern on the back of the square and trace the pattern lightly on the right side of the square.

Cut the reverse paper pattern piece for the back portion of the blanket. Press the pattern to the wrong side of the blanket fabric.

Prepare the piece for the background square by cutting it with a ¼" turn-under allowance.

While the paper pattern is still attached, use a light box to mark the overlaps lightly on the right side of the fabric (Figure 2).

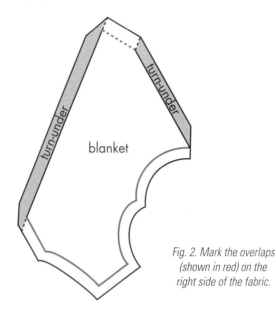

Fig. 2. Mark the overlaps (shown in red) on the right side of the fabric.

Dab starch and turn allowances under, leaving the allowances unturned where they will be overlapped by the tree branch and the baby.

Press allowances and glue the piece in place on the background square. Machine blind stitch the turned edges as follows: Trim the background from under the blanket. Next, turn the edges of the tree limb. Machine blind stitch close to the folded edges. Repeat with the leaves.

MACHINE APPLIQUÉ, BLIND STITCH:
Set your machine to blind stitch with a very narrow "bite." Let the foot ride on the background fabric, close to the appliqué (Figure 3). If your thread shows too much, you can try using invisible thread. If you're unsure of this technique, you may want to practice with a scrap.

Fig. 3. The "bite" of the blind stitch should barely show.

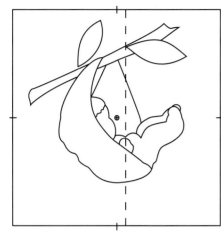

MORE OVERLAPS:

The baby's face has three overlaps: under the hair, the body, and the blanket. Leave these overlaps unturned. To avoid confusion, use a light box to mark the overlaps lightly.

Starch, turn, and press the remaining edges. Blind stitch the turned edges on the background square. Cut away the background fabric under the face.

Repeat with the hair, leg, body, hand, and the little part of the sleeve that shows. Take note of where the overlaps are, stitching each section as you go. Cut away the background in the larger areas. The final step is to appliqué the front of the blanket where there are no overlaps.

Press and trim the block to 12½".

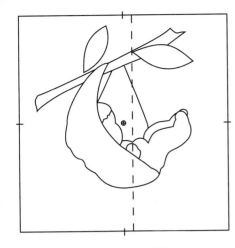

Cut templates on solid lines.
Add ¼" turn-under allowances,
by eye, as you cut fabric pieces.

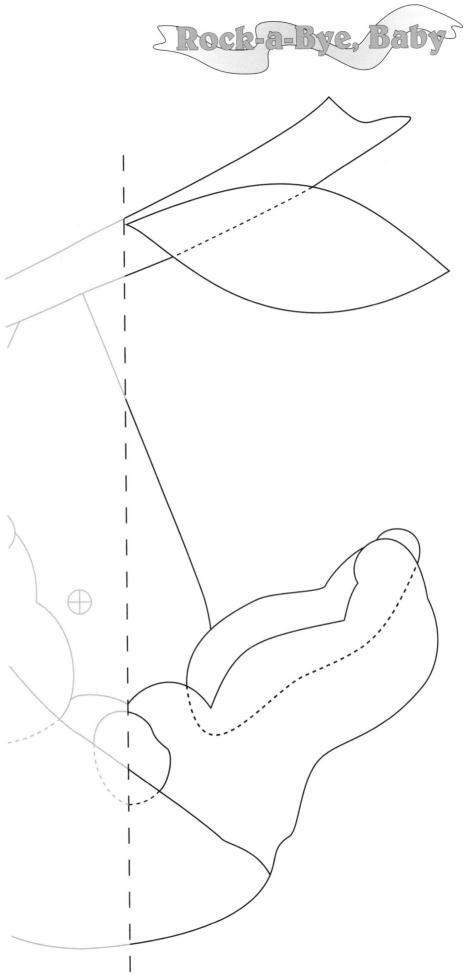

Little Boy Blue

Little boy blue,

Come blow your horn.

The sheep's in the meadow,

The cow's in the corn.

Where is the boy

That looks after the sheep?

He's under the haystack,

Fast asleep.

Lesson 5
HAND BUTTONHOLE STITCH
APPLIQUÉ FROM TOP TO BOTTOM
HAND EMBROIDERY

Techniques to Use
General Instructions (pages 7–8)
Preparing freezer paper whole pattern
Preparing background square
Preparing reverse pattern for appliqués
Starch and turn method

Lesson 1 (pages 11–12)
Turning allowances
Blind stitch by hand

Make a whole and a reverse pattern on 12" squares of freezer paper. Make separate reverse patterns of the haystack and the partially covered leg.

Cut a 14" fabric square for the background. Press the reverse pattern on the back of the square and trace the pattern lightly on the right side of the square.

Press the haystack pattern on the back of the haystack fabric. Cut out the haystack, including allowances. Turn under the haystack allowances, clipping into the inside corners. Glue the piece in position on the background square and appliqué it with a buttonhole stitch. Trim away the background square from under the haystack.

HAND BUTTONHOLE STITCH:
Use an embroidery hoop and one or two strands of embroidery thread that match the appliqué piece. Form tiny stitches that are about 1⁄16" deep, as shown.

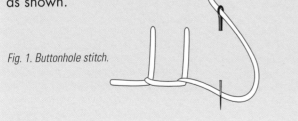

Fig. 1. Buttonhole stitch.

Cut the reverse pattern pieces apart and press them on the backs of the appropriate fabrics. Cut out the fabric pieces including turn-under allowance. Trace

all the overlaps on the right sides of the fabrics. Be sure to leave an overlap where the boy's hair is covered by his ear. Clip into the ear's allowances to bring the ear on top of the hair, then turn under the ear's allowances. Turn the rest of the allowances under.

Assemble the boy from top to bottom using the blind stitch and matching thread as described in the box below. After appliquéing the figure to the haystack, trim haystack fabric from beneath the boy. Place the completed square in an embroidery hoop and hand embroider the eyes, eyebrows, nose, and mouth.

Press and trim the block to 12½".

APPLIQUÉ FROM TOP TO BOTTOM:
The pieces for the boy will be appliquéd together before he is appliquéd to the haystack. You will be working from the top piece to the bottom one, as follows: Appliqué the hair to the face and the head to the body, then the arm to the hand, the shirt to the pants, and the pants to the stockings. Appliqué the top foot to the stockings. Appliqué the outer edges of the boy in place on the haystack, slipping the horn under the hand.

HAND EMBROIDERY:
Using two to three strands of brown embroidery floss, embroider the eyes, eyebrows, and nose with the outline stitch.

Fig. 2. Outline stitch.

Use two or three strands of dark pink embroidery floss for the mouth, and hand satin stitch as shown.

Fig. 3. Satin-stitched mouth.

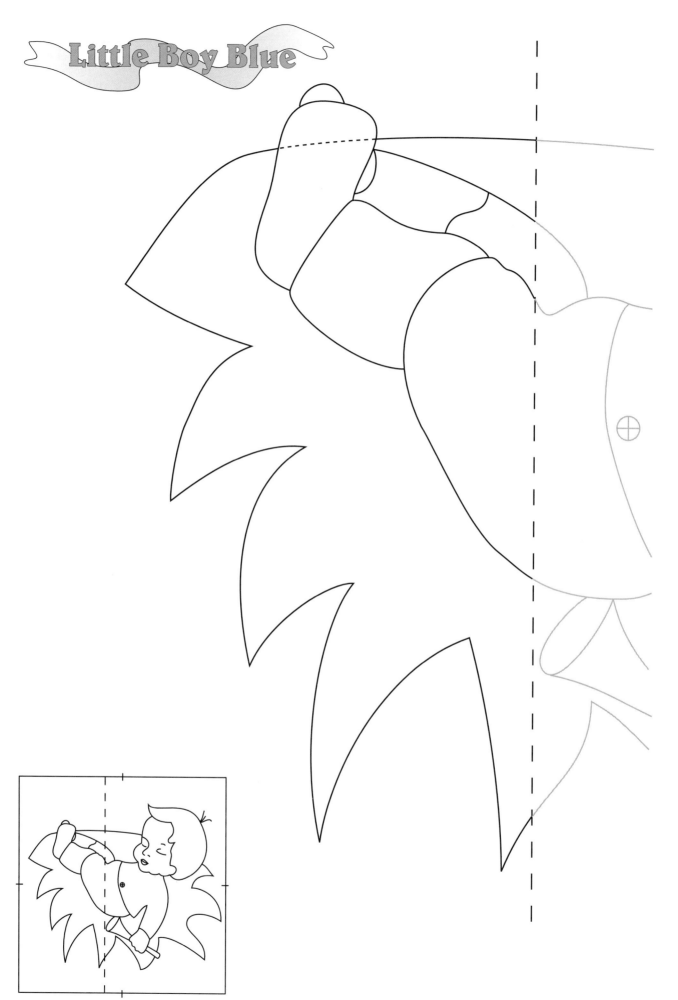

Rhyme Time Blocks 🙟 Rita Denenberg

Cut templates on solid lines.
Add ¼" turn-under allowances,
by eye, as you cut fabric pieces.

Humpty Dumpty

Humpty Dumpty
Sat on a wall.
Humpty Dumpty
Had a great fall.
All the King's horses
And all the King's men
Couldn't put Humpty Dumpty
Together again.

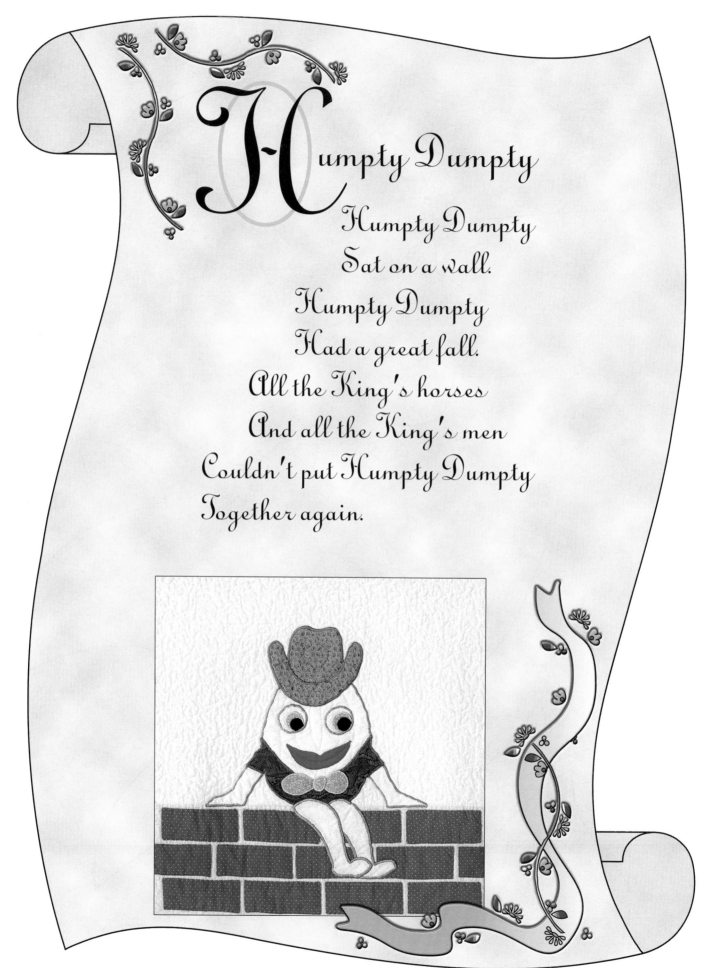

Lesson 6
RUNNING-STITCH APPLIQUÉ

Techniques to Use
General Instructions (pages 7–8)
Preparing freezer paper whole pattern
Preparing background square
Preparing reverse pattern for appliqués
Starch and turn method

Lesson 1 (page 11)
Turning allowances

Lesson 2 (page 16)
Perfect circles

Make a whole and a reverse pattern on 12" squares of freezer paper. Make separate reverse patterns of the legs.

Cut a 14" fabric square for the background. Press the reverse pattern on back of the square and lightly trace the wall and the egg on the right side of the fabric.

Cut the brick wall as one piece from the reverse pattern. Press the pattern on the wrong side of a piece of fabric that resembles mortar. The bricks will be appliquéd on top of the piece. Cut out the wall, adding 1" on the sides and bottom and ¼" on the top as you cut.

Trace the placement of the bricks on the right side of the wall and number the bricks on the whole pattern (Figure 1).

Fig. 1. Number each brick on the whole pattern.

Turn under the allowance along the top edge of the wall and blind stitch that edge in place on the background square. Cut away the background square, ¼" from the stitching, underneath the wall.

Remove the reverse pattern and cut the bricks from the pattern, cutting through the legs for bricks 2, 3, 7, and 8. Press the bricks to the wrong side of the fabric and cut the bricks with a ¼" turn-under allowance.

Mark each fabric brick with its number. Turn under the corners of the allowances, then turn under the sides.

Cut the remaining pieces from the reverse pattern. Leave the shirt and sleeves as one piece and the hat and brim as one piece.

Press the reverse patterns for the arms on the wrong side of the fabric. Cut out the arms with allowances. Turn under all the edges except the top one for the overlap. Blind stitch the arms on the background square.

Use the reverse pattern to cut the shirt from the fabric. On the fabric, mark the shoulder sleeve lines, which can be quilted. Mark the overlaps. Turn and press the allowances, leaving the overlaps unturned. Blind stitch the shirt to the background square.

Use the reverse pattern to cut the head from fabric. Turn all the edges except for the top, which will be overlapped by the hat. Blind stitch the head to the background with a blind stitch. Add the hat and the tie in the same manner.

Add the legs, one at a time, noting the overlap on the partially covered leg. Blind stitch in place. Cut away the background from under the large pieces.

Add the eyes by using the perfect circles method. Cut the mouth as one piece, tracing the line in the center for quilting.

Press and trim the block to 12½".

RUNNING-STITCH APPLIQUÉ:
Glue-stick the bricks in place on the wall and use a running stitch to attach (Figure 2). All the other appliqué pieces will be blind stitched.

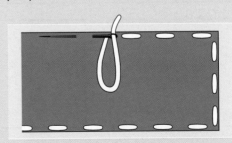

Fig. 2. The running stitch goes through all the layers. Keep the stitches close to the edge and even.

Humpty Dumpty

Rhyme Time Blocks ~ *Rita Denenberg*

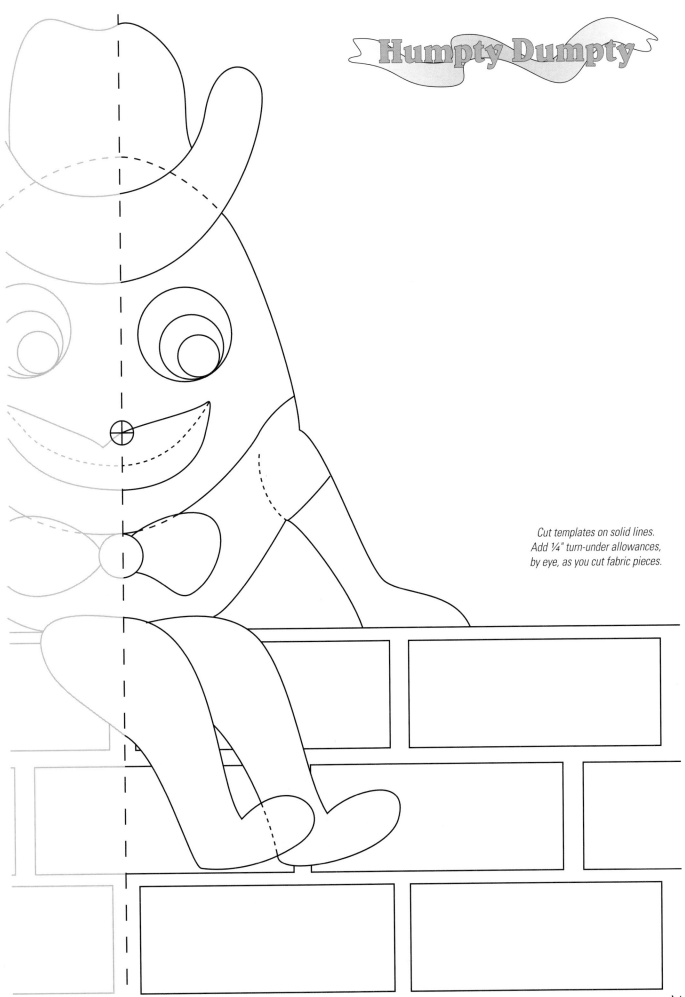

Humpty Dumpty

Cut templates on solid lines.
Add ¼" turn-under allowances,
by eye, as you cut fabric pieces.

Old Woman in a Shoe

There was an old woman
Who lived in a shoe.
She had so many children,
She didn't know what to do.
She gave them some broth
Without any bread;
She whipped them all soundly
And sent them to bed.

Lesson 7
REVERSE APPLIQUÉ

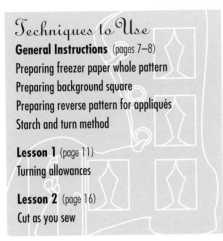
Make a whole and a reverse pattern on 12" squares of freezer paper.

Cut a 14" fabric square for the background. Press the reverse pattern on the back of the square and trace the shoe outline lightly on the right side of the square.

REVERSE APPLIQUÉ:

With this method, fabrics are layered, and the top layers are cut away to expose the fabric underneath.

Cut a 12" black fabric square. Transfer your whole pattern to this square. If you can't see the pattern through the black fabric with a light source, you can use dressmaker's "carbons" to transfer the design.

Cut one rectangle (2¾" by 2⅝") from each of the pastel colors, yellow, green, blue, and pink. Trace the curtains on the right side of these rectangles.

With the pastels on top, stab pins straight down through the curtain corners and into the window corners on the black shoe to avoid shifting. Pin the pastels in place and remove stab pins.

Use the cut-as-you-sew method for turning the inside edges of curtains to expose the black fabric (Figure 1).

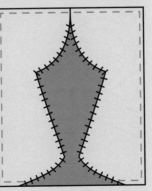

Fig. 1. Appliqué inside edge of curtain to expose black fabric. Leave outside allowances unturned.

Match the center of the black square to the center of the background square; baste.

Use the cut-as-you-sew method to appliqué only the portion of the black shoe that will extend beyond the upper part of the brown shoe, as shown in Figure 2. Cut the rest of the black shoe on the line; add turn-under allowance only below the door frame.

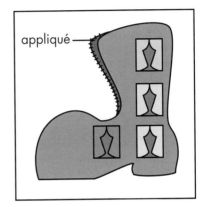

Fig. 2. Appliqué the front edge of the black shoe.

Cut the pieces for the woman from the reverse pattern. Press them on the backs of the appropriate fabrics and cut out the fabric pieces with ¼" turn-under allowances. Turn under all the allowances, leaving the overlaps unturned. Blind stitch the pieces for the woman in place. Do not appliqué her hand yet.

Trace the whole shoe pattern on the right side of a 12" square of brown shoe fabric. You need to transfer only the shoe outline, window outlines, and the door opening and placement.

Match the centers of the brown square and the black shoe. Drop pins into corners of windows and doors, matching those underneath, and pin in place; baste. Cut away ¼" of drawn line to expose windows and door opening. Clip to corners, stitch using blind hem stitch, turning in black for door opening. Use the cut-as-you-sew method to appliqué the shoe outline. In the same manner, carefully cut and sew the outlines of the windows and the door.

Fig. 3. Cut reverse patterns for the door and the edge.

Cut away the background fabric from underneath the shoe.

Cut out the reverse patterns of the door and the door's edge, shown in yellow in Figure 3.

Press the reverse door pattern to the wrong side of the brown fabric and cut the door with turn-under allowances. Turn and press all the allowances.

Press the reverse door edge pattern to the appropriate fabric and lightly draw the overlap line on the front of the fabric. Align the left edge of the door with the overlap line on the edge piece. Appliqué the door to the edge piece along the line.

Trim the edge piece allowance to within ¼" of the stitching. Trim the three remaining edges, leaving a ¼" allowance. Turn under the allowances, clipping

as needed to keep the strip from showing beyond the door. Appliqué the woman's hand to the door. Then appliqué the door in place.

Trace three circles for the eyelets. Appliqué the outer edges in place. Carefully trim the inside of the eyelets and the brown fabric close to the appliquéd stitches, exposing the black. Blind stitch inside edges of the circles.

Appliqué the laces to the shoe. Embroider the door knob.

Press and trim the block to 12½".

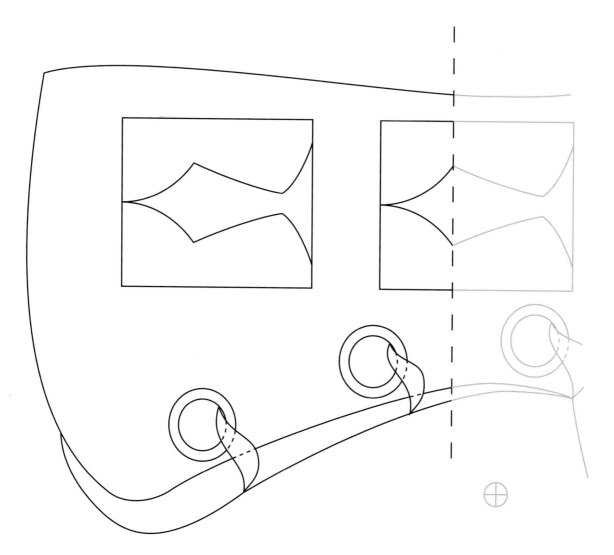

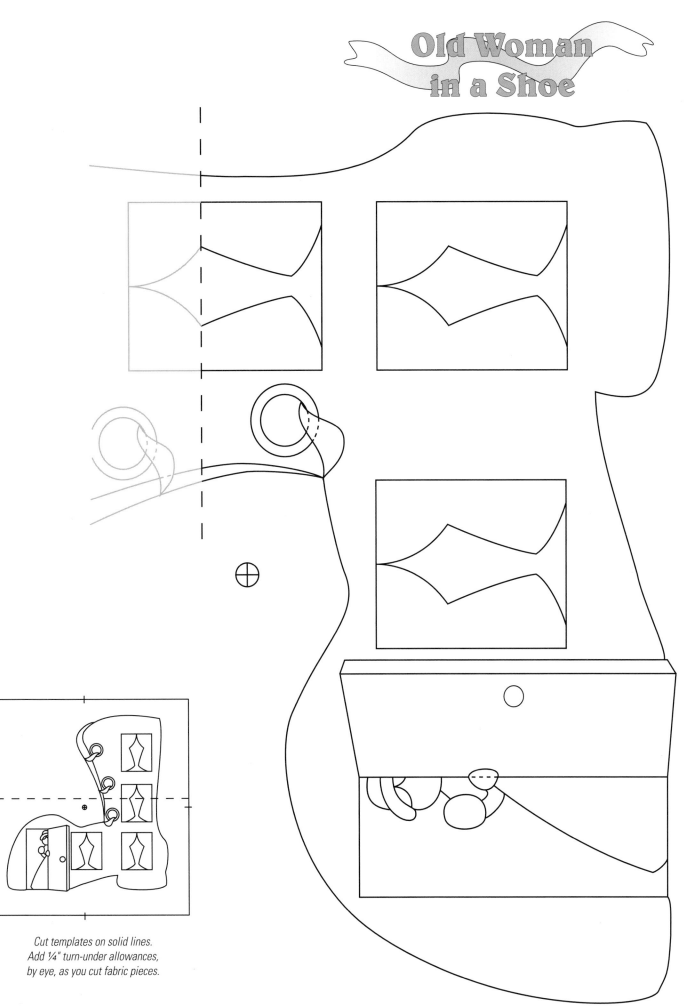

Cut templates on solid lines.
Add ¼" turn-under allowances,
by eye, as you cut fabric pieces.

Baa, Baa, Black Sheep

Baa, baa, black sheep
Have you any wool?
Yes sir, yes sir,
Three bags full.
One for my master
One for my dame,
And one for the little boy
Who lives down the lane.

Lesson 8
SATIN RIBBON (optional)
MACHINE BLANKET STITCH

Make a whole and a reverse pattern on 12" squares of freezer paper. Make an extra reverse pattern of the ball of yarn.

Cut a 14" fabric square for the background. Press the reverse pattern on the back of the square and trace the pattern lightly on the right side of the square.

Cut the reverse pattern pieces apart. Press them on the wrong sides of the appropriate fabrics and cut the pieces, adding ¼" turn-under allowances by eye as you cut.

Mark quilting lines on the ball of yarn. Turn the allowance under and blind stitch the ball in place on the background square. Cut away the background fabric from under the ball. Appliqué the yarn pieces with a blind stitch.

SATIN RIBBON:
If you want to substitute double-sided satin ribbon for the yarn fabric, twist the ribbon as you see in the photograph. Place the ribbon so the outside edges lie flat. Blind stitch in place, easing the inside curves. You don't want any loose ribbon for baby to get caught in.

Turn the allowances on the sheep's legs that are partially covered, leaving the overlaps unturned. Machine blanket stitch the legs in place. Repeat with the bodies, heads, and faces. The eyes can be embroidered.

Press and trim the block to 12½".

MACHINE BLANKET STITCH:
If you are fortunate enough to have this stitch on your machine, it can produce a nice, clean effect (Figure 1). Use invisible thread in your needle and cotton thread in the bobbin. Keep the stitch length and width about ¹⁄₁₆".

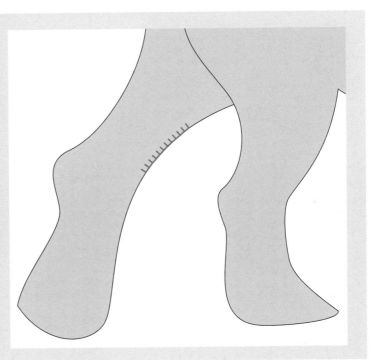

Fig. 1. Machine blanket stitch.

Baa, Baa,
Black Sheep

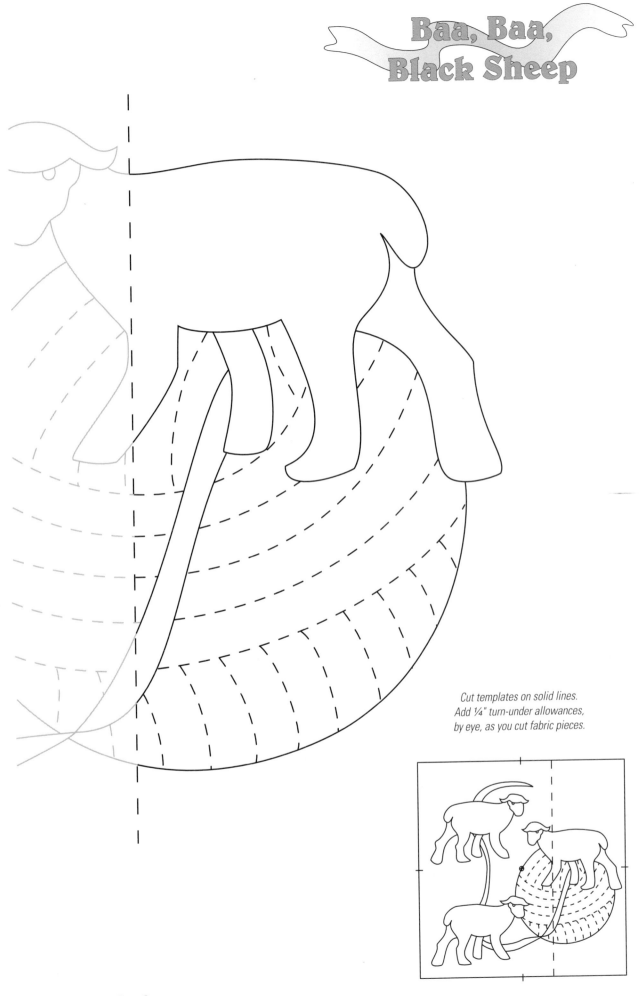

Cut templates on solid lines.
Add ¼" turn-under allowances,
by eye, as you cut fabric pieces.

Pussycat, Pussycat

Pussycat, pussycat,
Where have you been?
"I've been to London
To look at the queen."
Pussycat, pussycat,
What did you there?
"I frightened a little mouse
Under the chair."

Lesson 9
LESS TRACING
NARROW ENCLOSED STRIPS

LESS TRACING:

The following appliqué method requires less tracing than other methods.

Make a whole and a reverse pattern on 12" squares of freezer paper. Make separate reverse patterns for the scepter and the tie for the cape.

Cut a 14" fabric square for the background. Press the reverse pattern on the back of the square. Mark the corners of the 12" square on the back of the background square. Remove the pattern.

Carefully cut out the whole cat from the reverse pattern. Press the pattern, minus the cat, on the back of the background square, matching the corners of the square to the corner marks. If you place the background square, right side up, on a light box, you will see the outline of the cat. There is no need to trace anything on the background square. The cat outline revealed by the light will show you where to place the appliqués (Figure 1).

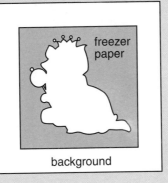

Fig. 1. Use the reverse pattern as a placement guide.

Mark the location of the turn-under allowances on the reverse cat pattern (Figure 2). Press the pattern to the wrong side of a gray fabric and cut the cat, adding ¼" turn-under allowances by eye as you cut in the marked areas. Cut the rest of the cat on the drawn line. Turn the allowances under, clipping where necessary.

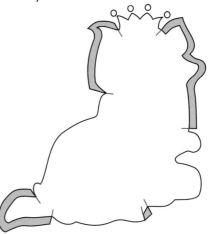

Fig. 2. Mark turn-under allowances, shown in red. Allowances are blue. Cut the rest of the cat on the pattern outline.

Do not remove the entire pattern, but carefully snip the inner part of the ears (pink in the photo) from the pattern. Re-press the pattern to the back of the cat.

With the cat pattern face up over a light source, trace the inner part of the ears on the gray cat. Remove the cat pattern.

Cut two pieces of pink fabric, each one large enough to contain the inner-ear pattern plus allowances. Press the reverse inner-ear patterns on the wrong side of the pink fabric pieces.

Using a light box, place the pink pieces, with the patterns still attached, under the cat's ears. Apply a glue stick to keep the pink pieces in place. Remove the inner-ear patterns from the pink fabric. From the front of the cat, use the cut-as-you-sew method to needle-turn the ears to reveal the pink underneath.

From the reverse cat pattern, carefully cut out the face, tummy, and paw 1 as one piece (Figure 3 on the following page). Re-press what remains of the reverse cat pattern to the back of the cat.

Press this pattern to the back of a white fabric. Trace paw 1 and the facial features on the front side of the fabric.

Fig. 3. Cut face, tummy, and paw 1 from the reverse pattern.

Keeping the paper pattern attached to the fabric, slip a small pair of scissors under the paw and cut it out to use for a pattern. If the lower portion of the pattern comes off, re-press the the paw in place to serve as a guide for replacing it. Then remove the paw pattern. The gap will show you where to sew paw 1 later.

Turn the allowances of the white piece and remove the paper. Place the cat, with its paper pattern still attached, right side up on a light source. You will see the space where the face, tummy, and paw were. Use this outline to place the prepared white section. Appliqué it in place and cut away the gray underneath.

Note: You have not attached anything to the background square yet, and you still have raw edges on the cat that have not been turned under. These raw edges will help you place the other appliqués.

Place the reverse freezer paper pattern for the crown on the back of the crown fabric and press. Cut the crown, adding ¼" turn-under allowances as you cut. Turn under the allowances, clipping into the V's where necessary. Glue in place, using the raw edges of the cat as guides.

Appliqué along the edge where the crown meets the head, then trim the gray from behind the crown, leaving a ¼" allowance.

Cut paws 2, 3, and 4 from the reverse pattern. Press the patterns on the wrong side of a dark gray fabric.

Cut ¼" around the paws. Mark the overlaps and turn the remaining edges; press.

Using a light source to position the pieces, use a glue stick to attach paws 2 and 4 to the cat. Appliqué the inside edge of paw 4 and cut away the gray fabric from behind the paw. Appliqué the inside edge of paw 1 to the tummy.

NARROW ENCLOSED STRIPS:

You will need a narrow strip for the scepter. The easiest way to make one is to cut a bias strip 6" long and a scant ¾" wide. Fold the strip in half lengthwise and press. Draw a line ³⁄₁₆" from the folded edge. Machine baste on the line (Figure 4).

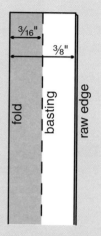

Fig. 4. Machine baste on the drawn line.

With the fold on the left, use a light box to position the strip on the background square. Align the basted line with the left side of the scepter. Make sure you have allowed for the overlap of the ball. Remove the paper pattern from the cat.

Carefully pull paw 2 to release it from the glue. Push the paw to the side and, with the machine, sew along the basted line. Trim the raw edges close to the stitching (Figure 5). Turn the folded edge to the right. Blind stitch in place (Figure 6).

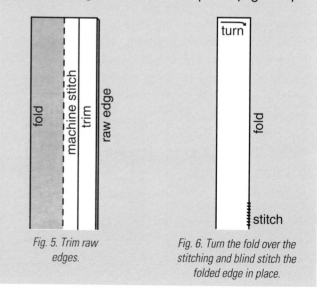

Fig. 5. Trim raw edges.

Fig. 6. Turn the fold over the stitching and blind stitch the folded edge in place.

You cannot attach paw 2 yet because the scepter has to be placed behind it. Make sure you have enough glue to hold the paw in place while you sew the other pieces. The glued paw can then be gently pulled away to add the scepter.

Cut the lower portion of the tummy (gray in the photo) from the reverse pattern and prepare the piece for appliquéing. Appliqué the lower portion of the tummy and paw 3 in place. Trim away the gray fabric from behind these pieces.

Place the background square, with the reverse pattern still attached, right side up on a light source. Dab the cat on the back with a glue stick and place it on the background square. Appliqué all the turned edges except paw 2. Cut away the background fabric from under the cat.

From the extra reverse scepter pattern, cut the ball, adding a ¼" turn-under allowance as you cut. Turn the allowances and press. Set aside.

Finish appliquéing the paws. The remaining freezer-paper pattern is for the cape. Do not cut the ermine trim from the pattern, yet.

Press the reverse cape pattern on the wrong side of the cape fabric and, as previously, note the overlaps for the ermine trim and the tie. Add turn-under allowances where applicable; dab starch, turn, and press.

Carefully cut the ermine trim from the paper pattern and remove the patches (black in the photo). Press the trim pattern on the wrong side of a white fabric, add allowances and overlaps, turn the allowances, and press.

Press the patch patterns on the wrong side of a black fabric. Cut the ermine patches, adding allowances. Turn the allowances and press. While the paper pattern is still on the trim, place the piece over a light source. Use a glue stick to place the black patches in the appropriate places.

Remove all the papers and appliqué the black patches in place. Attach the trim to the cape, matching the raw edges. Cut away the back of the cape under the ermine trim. Match the cape to the raw edges of the cat and appliqué in place.

Cut the tie from the cape fabric, adding turn-under allowances as you cut. Turn the allowances and press. Appliqué the tie in place. Trim away the gray fabric underneath.

Your final steps are to attach the ball of the scepter and trim the fabric from underneath it. Use the perfect circles method, page 16, to add the circles to the scepter and the crown. Embroider the face with the satin stitch, and outline the eyes with black embroidery floss.

Press and trim the block to 12½".

Pussycat, Pussycat

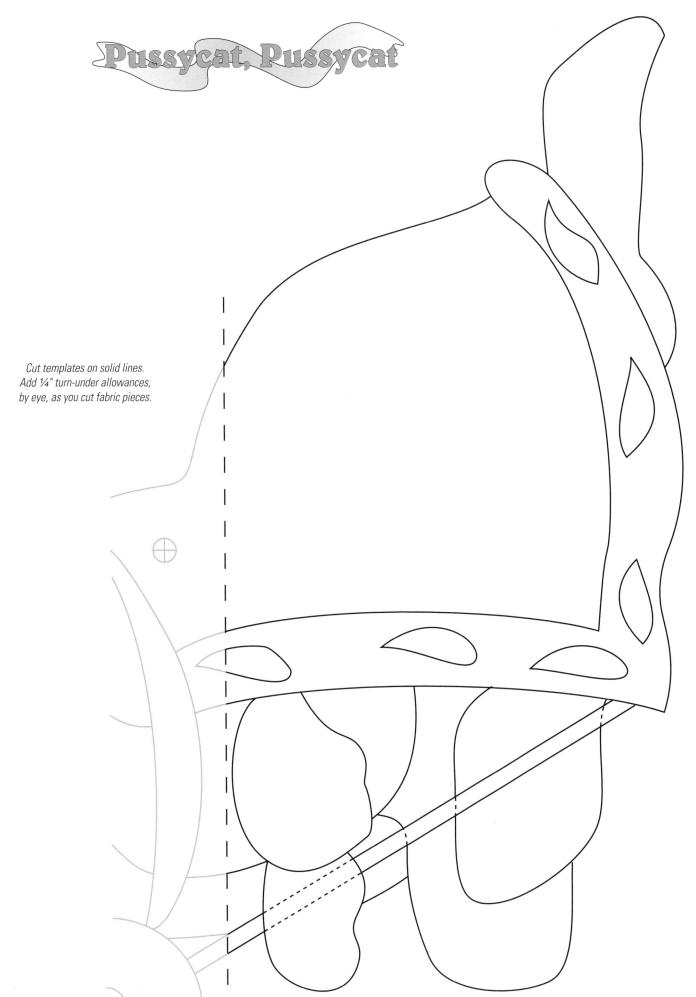

Cut templates on solid lines.
Add ¼" turn-under allowances,
by eye, as you cut fabric pieces.

Lesson 10

TRIMMING BLOCKS
QUILT SIZES
ASSEMBLING BLOCKS

TRIMMING BLOCKS:

Finger press each 14½" square in half, and in half again, to locate the center. Measuring 6¼" from the center creases, trim the blocks on all four sides to make a 12½" block, including seam allowances.

There are 12½" square rulers on the market that are handy for trimming the blocks, but you can make a template out of plastic template material or cardboard. If you make your own, draw lines across the center lengthwise and crosswise.

Regardless of which template you use, match the center lines of the template and the block. Mark the cutting lines in pencil and cut with scissors. It's best not to rotary cut because it's difficult to hold a ruler steady on an appliquéd block. You don't want to ruin the block with a bad cut.

QUILT SIZES:

If you are using twenty 12½" blocks with 1½" sashings and 1½" borders, as for the quilt in Figure 1, your finished quilt will be 58½" x 72". A typical baby's quilt is 36" x 54". Lap quilt dimensions are 54" x 72", and a twin is 54" x 90".

Fig. 1. Possible quilt setting for 20 blocks.

The quilt in Photo 1 shows how 15 blocks can be set together with sashing. You can even make a quilt from just one block to use as a wall decoration (Photo 2). Layer the block with batting and backing; quilt and bind it. Then sew a sleeve in back at the top. Insert a curtain rod in the sleeve and hang it on a couple of brackets in the wall.

To create a quilt of any size, you can use more or fewer blocks and set the blocks together with or without sashing, and the sashing can vary in width. You might add a border or several borders of any width. You could also use a photocopier to reduce or enlarge the block patterns. See page 15 for an example of a four-block quilt.

If you want to make a baby quilt, use three blocks across and five down without sashing (Figure 2).

There are two ways to make sashing, sometimes called lattice. A quilt with three 12" (finished) blocks across and three blocks down, plus 2" (finished) sashings will result in a quilt 44" square (Figure 3, page 58). You could add cornerstones to the sashing, if you want (Figure 4, page 58).

Fig. 2. Create a baby quilt with 15 blocks.

For the wallhanging in Figure 4, make nine blocks of your choice and trim blocks to 12½". Cut 24 rectangles 2½" x 12½" and 16 cornerstones 2½" x 2½". For each block row, sew four sashing strips alternated with three blocks. Make three block rows. For each sashing row, alternate four cornerstones and three sashing strips. Make four sashing rows. Sew the block and sashing rows together to complete the quilt top.

Photo 1. Nursery Rhymes

Photo 2. THE CAT AND THE FIDDLE wallhanging by Mickie Swall.

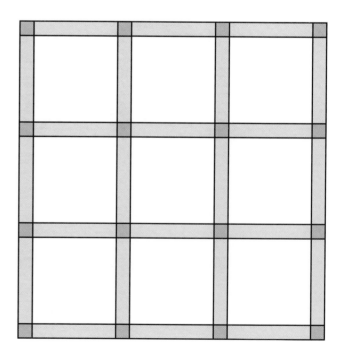

Fig. 3. Make a 44" square wallhanging with sashing.

Fig. 4. Cornerstones can be added to sashing.

$\mathscr{P}$art 3   More Patterns

Three Blind Mice

Three blind mice,
See how they run.
They all ran after
The farmer's wife,
Who cut off their tails
With a carving knife.
Did you ever see
Such a thing in your life
As three blind mice?

Three Blind Mice

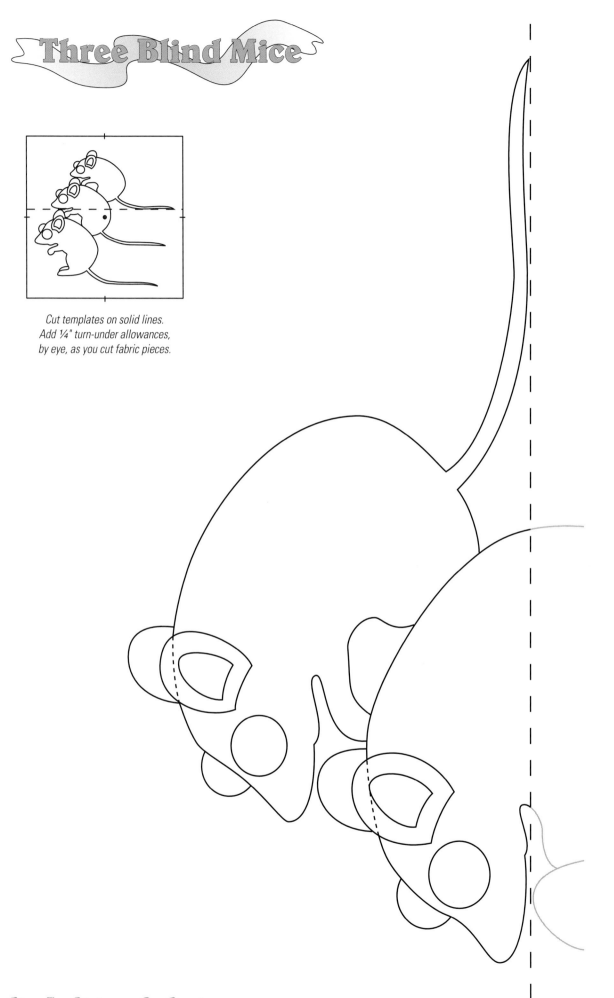

Cut templates on solid lines.
Add ¼" turn-under allowances,
by eye, as you cut fabric pieces.

Three Blind Mice

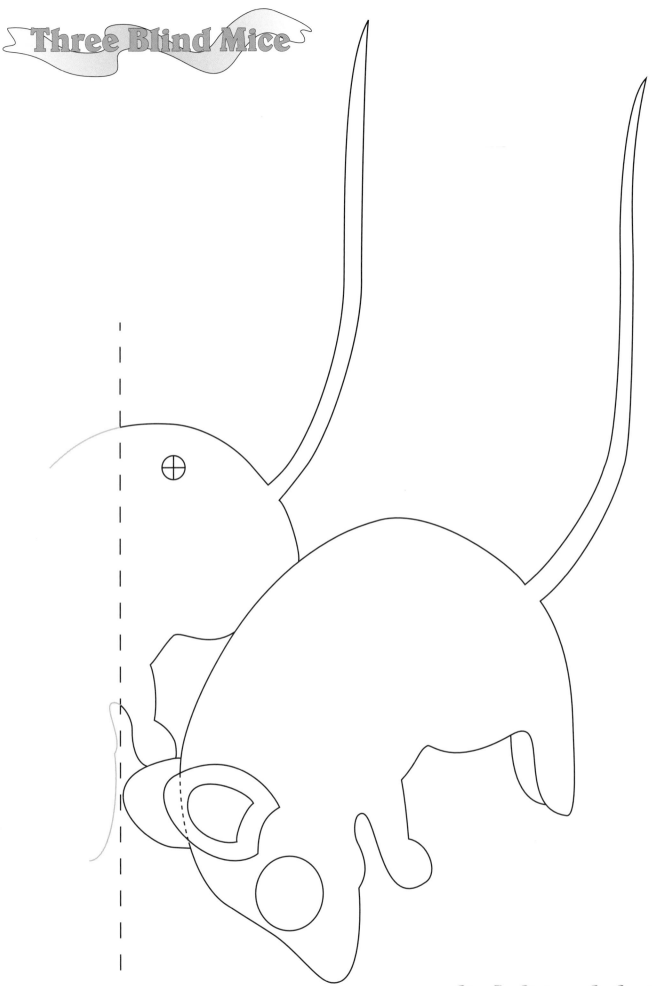

Jack and Jill

Jack and Jill
Went up the hill
To fetch a pail of water.
Jack fell down
And broke his crown,
And Jill came tumbling after.

Jack and Jill

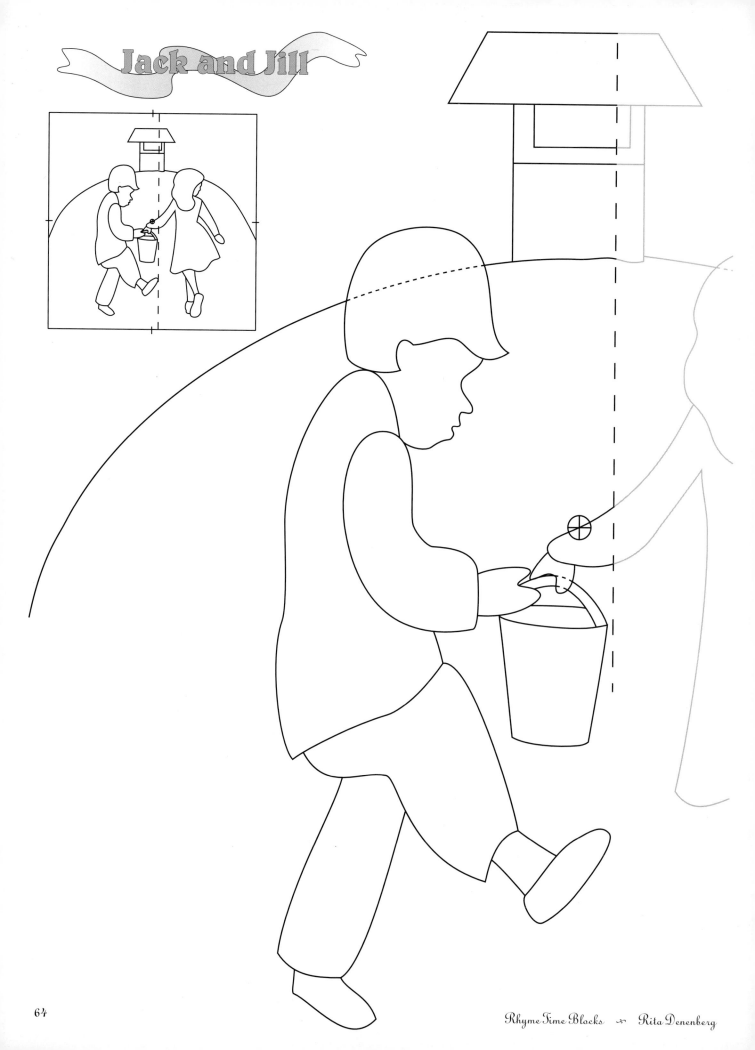

Rhyme Time Blocks ❧ *Rita Denenberg*

Jack and Jill

Cut templates on solid lines.
Add ¼" turn-under allowances,
by eye, as you cut fabric pieces.

Three Little Kittens

Three little kittens,
They lost their mittens,
And they began to cry,
Oh, mother, dear, we sadly fear
Our mittens we have lost.
What! Lost your mittens?
You naughty kittens.
Then you shall have no pie.

The three little kittens,
They found their mittens,
And they began to cry,
Oh, mother, dear,
We found our mittens.
Then you're good kittens,
And you shall have some pie.
Purrr, purrr
Then you shall have some pie.

Three Little Kittens

Cut templates on solid lines.
Add ¼" turn-under allowances,
by eye, as you cut fabric pieces.

Little Jack Horner

Little Jack Horner
Sat in the corner,
Eating his Christmas pie.
He put in his thumb
And pulled out a plum
And said, "What a good boy am I."

Little Jack Horner

Little Jack Horner

Cut templates on solid lines.
Add ¼" turn-under allowances,
by eye, as you cut fabric pieces.

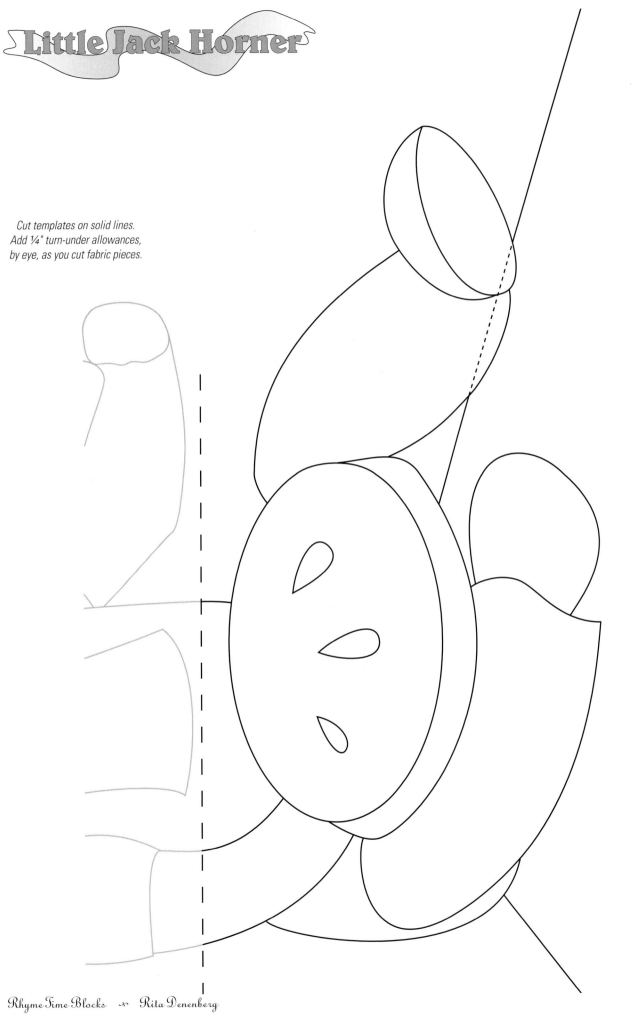

Little Miss Muffet

Little Miss Muffet
Sat on a tuffet,
Eating her curds and whey.
Along came a spider
And sat down beside her
And frightened Miss Muffet away.

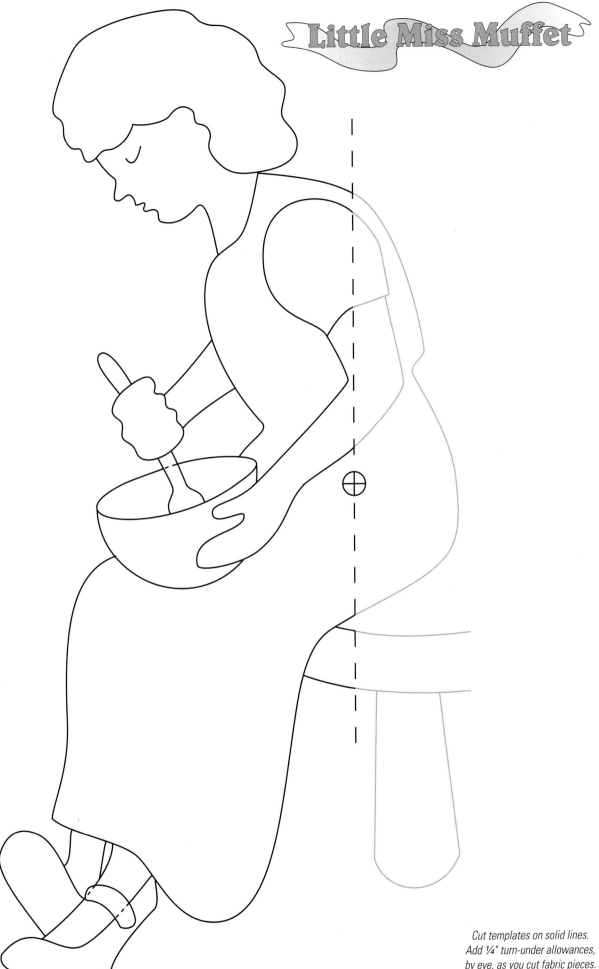

Little Miss Muffet

*Cut templates on solid lines.
Add ¼" turn-under allowances,
by eye, as you cut fabric pieces.*

Rhyme Time Blocks ⁓ Rita Denenberg

73

Little Miss Muffet

Rhyme Time Blocks ❧ Rita Denenberg

Mary Had a Little Lamb

Mary had a little lamb.

Its fleece was white as snow.

And everywhere that Mary went,

The lamb was sure to go.

He followed her to school one day,

That was against the rule.

It made the children laugh and play

To see a lamb at school.

Mary Had a Little Lamb

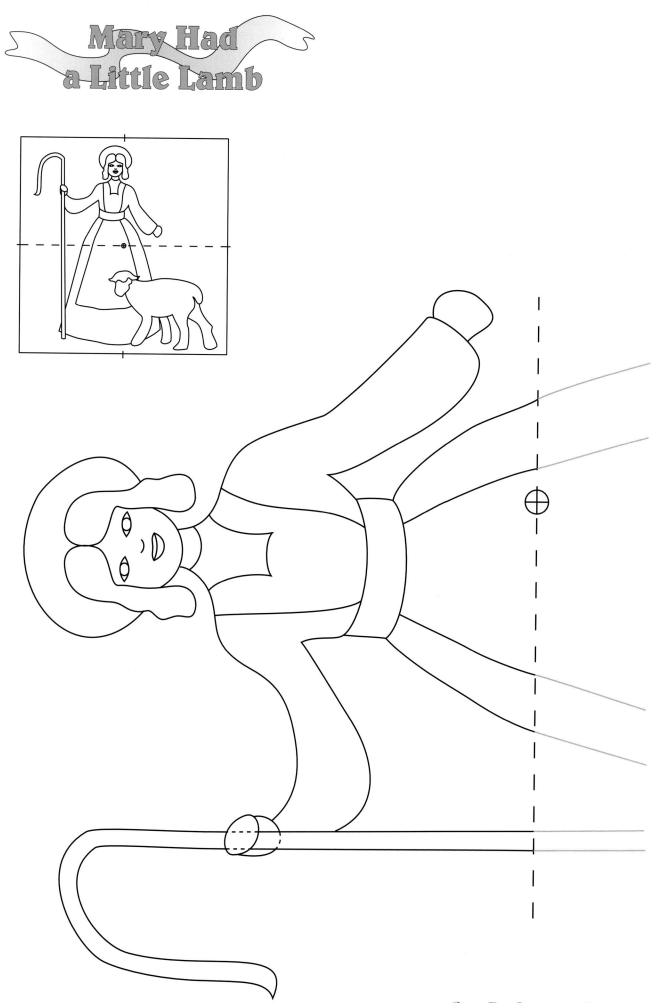

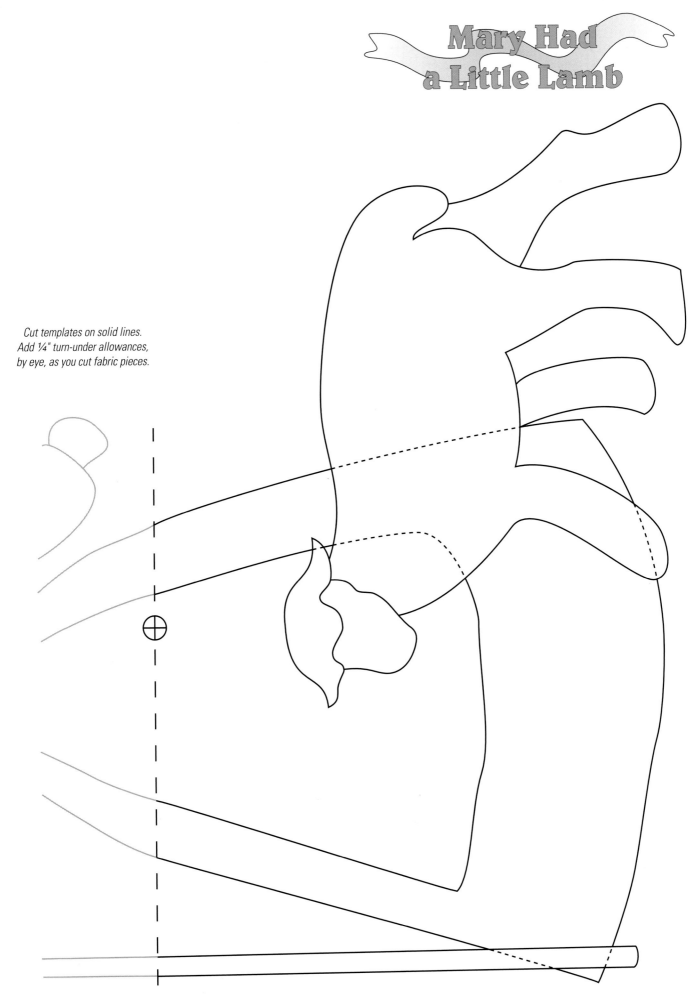

Cut templates on solid lines.
Add ¼" turn-under allowances,
by eye, as you cut fabric pieces.

Old King Cole

Old King Cole was a merry old soul,
And a merry old soul was he.
He called for his pipe,
And he called for his bowl,
And he called for his fiddlers three.

Cut templates on solid lines.
Add ¼" turn-under allowances,
by eye, as you cut fabric pieces.

Old King Cole

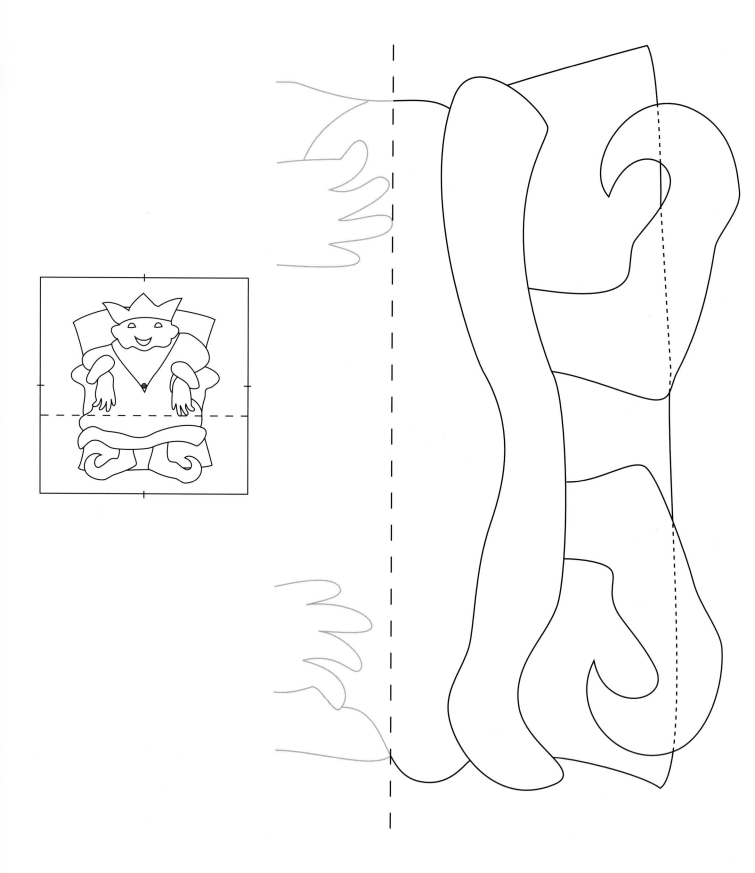

This Little Piggy

This little piggy went to market.
This little piggy stayed home.
This little piggy had roast beef.
This litttle piggy had none.
This little piggy cried, "Wee, wee, wee,"
All the way home.

This Little Piggy

Cut templates on solid lines.
Add ¼" turn-under allowances,
by eye, as you cut fabric pieces.

M A R K E T

T A

This Little Piggy

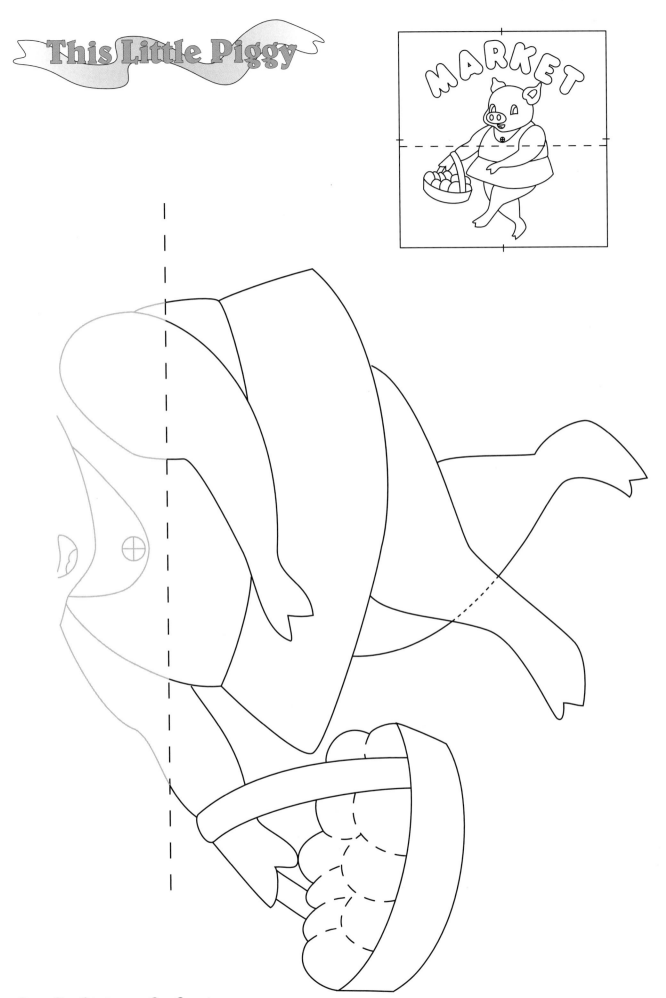

MARKET

Mother Goose

Old Mother Goose,
When she wanted to wander,
Would ride through the air
On a very fine gander.

Cut templates on solid lines.
Add ¼" turn-under allowances,
by eye, as you cut fabric pieces.

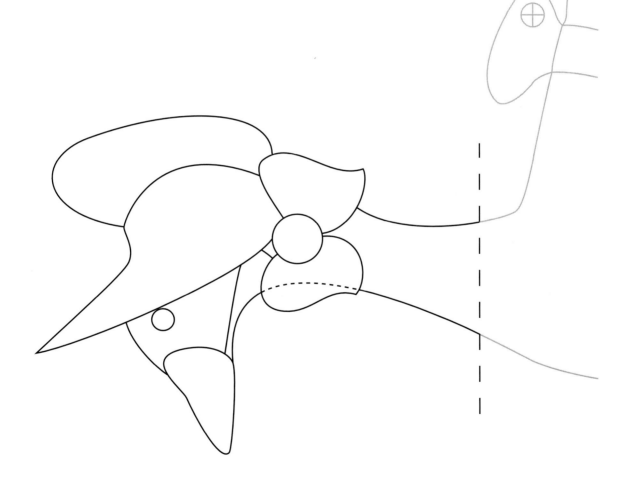

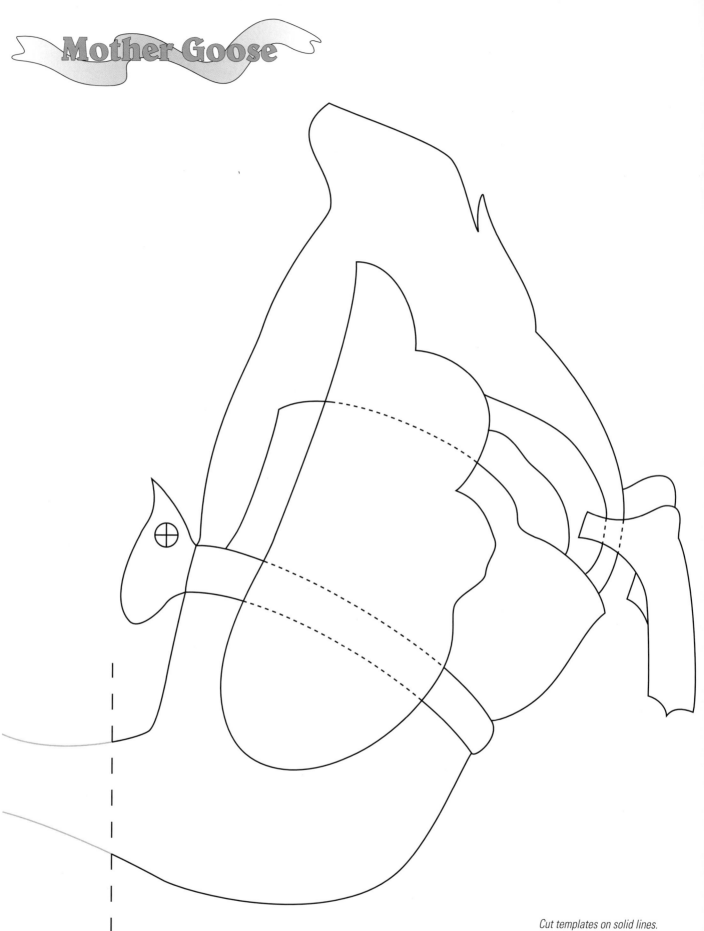

Cut templates on solid lines.
Add ¼" turn-under allowances,
by eye, as you cut fabric pieces.

About the Author

Rita Denenberg started learning to embroider at age 5 when her stepmother punched holes in some of Rita's drawings for her to outline stitch. By age 6, she was embroidering on fabric. By age 10, she had taught herself to sew by machine.

Rita loved her art classes in school, and by age 13 had won several awards, including a four-year art scholarship to a school in Manhattan, too far from home for a young girl. Undaunted, she continued to draw and sew.

Rita kept using her sewing skills after she married. She made decorative pieces for her house, such as slipcovers and drapes, and she made clothing for her five children. She also held several positions throughout the years as a tailor, making alterations and sewing garments in factories. She also freelanced as an artist, teaching herself oil painting, watercolor, and etching, and won many awards in the field. Rita also taught adult classes in oil painting.

About 1982, Rita saw a television show on quilting, and she was intrigued enough to make a wallhanging. Having developed allergies to various painting media which stopped her from painting, she discovered that quilting fulfilled her need for artistic expression, and she was thrilled with the opportunity to combine art and sewing.

By reading books, she taught herself the craft of quilt-making, and proceeded to make utilitarian patchwork quilts for herself and family members. Her beginning quilts were pieced and appliquéd by hand and hand quilted on a frame. Now, she primarily uses the sewing machine for all her quilt work.

An award-winning designer and quilter, she has had a quilt juried into the American Quilter's Society Show every year since 1988 and won second place in appliqué in 1990. She both teaches and lectures on quilting, and many of her appliqué patterns can be found in computer quilt design programs.

Part 4   Coloring Pages

Humpty Dumpty sat on a wall...

There was an old woman who lived in a shoe...

Rhyme Time Blocks ✂ Rita Denenberg

Pussycat, pussycat, where have you been?

Everywhere that Mary went, the lamb was sure to go

Rhyme Time Blocks ✎ Rita Denenberg

The cow jumped over the moon.

Jack and Jill went up the hill...

This is only a small selection of the books available from the American Quilter's Society. AQS books are known worldwide for timely topics, clear writing, beautiful color photos, and accurate illustrations and patterns. The following books are available from your local bookseller, quilt shop, or public library.

Quilted Havens CITY HOUSES, COUNTRY HOMES
Susan Purney-Mark & Daphne Greig
#5336 $22.95

Love to Quilt... Historical **Penny Squares**
Embroidery Patterns With Sampuenuie
#4753 $12.95

Love to Quilt **Petal by Petal** Appli-bond Flowers
Joan Shay
#5013 $14.95

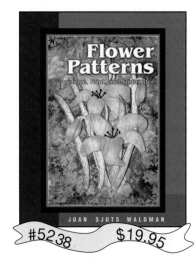

Flower Patterns To Applique, Paint, and Embroider
JOAN SJUTS WALDMAN
#5238 $19.95

THE BEST OF **JACOBEAN APPLIQUE**
Patricia B. Campbell & Mimi Ayars, Ph.D.
Includes EXOTICA & ROMANTICA Patterns
#5588 $24.95

Love to Quilt **BEARS** Bears Bears
Karen Kay Buckley
#4815 $14.95

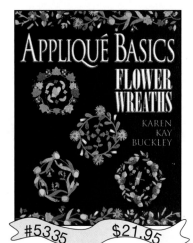

APPLIQUÉ BASICS FLOWER WREATHS
KAREN KAY BUCKLEY
#5335 $21.95

Stitch A Child's Quilt
Vicki M. A. Thomas
#5236 $18.95

Favorite **REDWORK DESIGNS**
BETTY ALDERMAN
#5331 $16.95

LOOK FOR THESE BOOKS NATIONALLY OR CALL   **1-800-626-5420**